THE BODY OF LANGUAGE

THE ITALIAN LIST

Giorgio Agamben

The Body of Language
esperruquancluzelubelouzerirelu

Translated by Kevin Attell

LONDON NEW YORK CALCUTTA

THE ITALIAN LIST

Series Editor: Alberto Toscano

This book has been translated thanks to a translation grant awarded by the Italian Ministry of Foreign Affairs and International Cooperation.

Questo libro è stato tradotto grazie a un contributo alla traduzione assegnato dal Ministero degli Affari Esteri e della Cooperazione Internazionale italiano.

Seagull Books, 2025

First published in Italian as *Il corpo della lingua*
© Giulio Einaudi editore s.p.a., Turin, 2024

First published in English translation by Seagull Books, 2025
English translation © Kevin Attell, 2025

ISBN 978 1 80309 476 2

British Library Cataloguing-in-Publication Data
A catalogue record for this book is available from the British Library

The original Italian edition, on which this edition is based,
was designed by Viviana Gottardello in collaboration with the author

Typeset by Diven Nagpal, Seagull Books, Calcutta, India

Est deus his venter, broda lex, ius inde vocatur.

For them the stomach is God, gravy is the law, that is why it is called *ius*.

Teofilo Folengo, *Baldo* (Toscolanense edition, 1521), BOOK 7, LINE 695.

Pourquoi en ce temps, non plus tard, print fin l'antique folie? Pourquoi en ce temps non plustost, commença la sagesse presente? Quel mal nous estoit de la folie precedente? Quel bien nous est de la sagesse succedente?

Why did its antecedent folly end now and not later? Why did its present wisdom begin now and not earlier? What ill did that antecedent folly do to us? And what good, the subsequent wisdom?

François Rabelais, Prologue to *Gargantua and Pantagruel*, BOOK 5.

Contents

I. The Body of Language 1
II. The Body of the Philosophers 45
III. Stultitia loquitur 65
IV. Self-Parody 85

Note on the Illustrations 102

Works Cited 103

Chapter One

The Body of Language

1. The human body becomes the measure of the world at the point where, exceeding all measure, it becomes truly boundless. Hurtaly, Pantagruel's giant ancestor and contemporary of the Flood, is too big to fit into the ark:

> He did sit astride it with a leg on either side like little children on their hobby-horses. In that way Hurtaly saved the aforesaid Ark from foundering, for he propelled it with his legs, turning it with his foot whichever way he would as one does with the rudder of a boat. (Rabelais, p. 21)

Pantagruel himself is so enormous that he cannot come to light without suffocating his mother Badebec, even though 68 mule drivers came out of her belly before him, each with a mule carrying a load of salt, and 9 dromedaries with a full burden of hams and smoked ox tongues—not to mention 7 camels loaded with eels and 25 carts full of leeks, garlic, onions and scallions. At every meal, the baby would drink the milk of 4,600 cows, and one day, when he managed to burst loose from his reins, he seized a cow by the hocks and 'bit off and ate her udders and half her belly' (p. 27). Once grown, his tongue is so huge that one can walk upon it for two leagues before entering the immense land of his mouth, where the teeth are 'huge rock formations like the mountains of Dent-mark', beyond which you can see 'wide meadows, great forests, and cities strong and spacious, no less big than Lyons or Poitiers' (p. 157). In two of these cities, called Larynx and Pharynx, there is currently a plague caused by 'stinking breath which had come out of Pantagruel's stomach after he had eaten so much garlic sauce' (p. 158). Proceeding in the direction of the ears, the forest is so dense that there are bands of brigands hiding ready to prey on any travellers who carelessly go too deep into the buccal land. 'I then began to think,' comments the author, Alcofribas Nasier,

> how true is the saying, 'One half of the world has no idea how the other half lives,' for nobody has ever written about those lands over yonder in which there are more than twenty-five inhabited kingdoms, not to mention deserts and a wide arm of sea. But I have compiled a thick book about them entitled *A History of the Gorgeous*—I have named them thus because they dwell in the *gorge* of Pantagruel my master. (Rabelais, pp. 158–59)

The first giant had made his entrance into literature almost seventy years earlier, in Pulci's *Morgante*, which, truth be told, is rather frugal in the description of its colossus, though it does let us know that he 'uproots pines, beeches, poplar trees, and oaks' and easily carries a horse over his shoulder (Pulci, p. 8). Much more detailed and imaginative is the description of the other giant, Margutte, who once wanted to be a giant but 'midway . . . was forced [his] dream to quit' and so remained only seven armlengths (about four meters) tall (p. 364). What is gigantic, however, is his roguery, at least as far as his gastronomic devotion is concerned:

> I less believe in what is black or blue
> than in a capon—boil or roast, who cares?
> And often I believe in butter, too,
> in beer and—every time I find it—must,
> which should be strong and genuine, not weak;
> yes, above all, I in good wine believe,
> for those who drink eternal life achieve. (p. 364)

It is well not to forget that the discovery of the body—the 'new place for human corporeality in the real spatial-temporal world', which Bakhtin opposes to medieval ascetic ideology—takes place in bodies that have burst out beyond their rightful size and surpassed their limits: bodies that are in every sense enormous and abnormal, that 'are aimed primarily at destroying the established hierarchy of values, at bringing down the high and raising up the low' (Bakhtin, pp. 170,

177). Bodies that are immense, in the etymological sense of the term: neither measured nor measurable. The bodies of giants, whose genealogy Rabelais meticulously traces, from Chalbroth to Gargantua, naming—among sixty others—Atlas, Goliath, Polyphemus, Sisyphus, Antaeus, Morgante (so he had read Pulci), Fracasso, 'whom Merlin Cocaio wrote about' (Rabelais, p. 20), all the way up to Garnet-cock and Grandgousier.

2. That Rabelais should name Merlin Cocaio, alias Teofilo Folengo of Mantua, is hardly surprising, given the influence exerted on him by the *Macaronei opus quod inscribitur Baldus*, published on 5 January 1521, *apud lacum benacense*, that is, on the shores of Lake Garda, where centuries later the late hunter Gracchus would land. From Folengo (a Benedictine monk, as Rabelais was a Franciscan) Rabelais learned to exalt another gigantic corporeality beyond the physiological, a corporeality that has to do not with the unrestrained excess of physical mass, but the prodigality and profligacy of language. Above all, in the literal sense, as when a character complains that for no reason someone has *morrambouzevezengouzequoquemorguatascabacguevezinemaffressé* (cowpatconked-windbagtrottled-thumptbumped-bangbong-shattered) his left eye, or another, battered with heavy fists, finds himself *esperruquancluzelubelouzerirelu* (maulocrippled-lowerhazarded) in his heel (Rabelais, p. 708). Pantagruel's language is as vast as his body. According to the philologists, in putting together words from the most varied jargons and dialects, Rabelais in some way tears down and transforms his language, at least as far as the lexicon is concerned (hence the need for the long glossaries at the end of his books and the publication in Germany of an improbable *Etymologisches Wörterbuch zu Rabelais*). His Mantuan teacher goes much further: he invents a language—*macaronicum* (or *macaron*, or even *macaronicon*)—and a poetic art that take their name from *macarones*, 'which are a type of dumpling made from

flour, cheese and butter, coarse, rough and rustic' (Folengo, *Le Maccheronee*, p. 284), since the 'joke-words' (*vocabolazzi*) that they employ must be just as course and rough. To be sure, the macaronic was invented *causa ridendi*, and if 'we say *se cagat addossum* [he beshits himself]', we do so 'to laugh, not to pray' (p. 285). But Folengo is fully aware of the operation he is performing on the body of the language. He knows that it is nothing less than, in defiance of the Dantean *exemplum*, giving a Latin body to the *vulgare eloquium* ('*quando quidem vulgare eloquium est macaronicis poetae latinizare*') and, conversely, vernacularizing Latin (p. 285). And just as Dante had walked through the woods of the dialects in search of the illustrious vernacular, so Folengo draws the material of the macaronic primarily from the dialects, which miraculously seem to be at his command.

When asked, 'O Merlin, you invent words that are only used in your region, like *doniare puellas, cimare, tracagnum*,' he calmly responds, 'Just as not everyone at once understands Greek, Hebrew, Arabic, Chaldean or even Latin, so one should not be surprised if not everyone understands Mantuan, Florentine, Bergamasque, German, Swiss, Slipperese or Chimneysweepese' (p. 285). And, in the end, it is critical that his transgression of the rules and boundaries of the languages is—or at least pretends to be—regulated: the *Normula macaronica de syllabis*, which concludes the Toscolanese edition (1521) of the poem, peremptorily states that 'all vernacular words that have been Latinized must be written in vernacular form, like *orecchia, occhius, rozzus, razza*, and so on.' And since the poem is written in hexameters, it is not merely out of fussiness that the *normula* specifies: 'as far as the Latin words go, they must retain their quantity, like *caballus, focus, accendo*, etc.' (p. 286). And macaronic words whose first syllable contains two consonants that are not joined to the second syllable—like *gridare, sbraiare, tracagnum*—can be considered long or short as one wishes; but if followed by a vowel, as in *briossus*, then the syllable is short.

3. To render the world corporeal through the excessiveness of the giants' limbs, then, goes hand in hand with the corporealization of language through their very speech, and it is more than likely that the first operation would not have been possible without the second,

which in reality is primitive in every sense. This also means that in the beginning was not the grammatical word, but a *verbocination* that, like that of the *eschollier*, flays both *nostre vernacule Gallique* and *la redonance latinicome* (Rabelais, pp. 34–36) or, as in Folengo (*Le Maccheronee*, p. 285), a *parlatio* made not of words but 'jokewords', which the cruder they become, the more they achieve 'macaronic elegance'. The parody of the Gospel of John that opens the *Morgante* ('In the beginning was the Word near God, / God was the Word, and so the Word was He: / this I believe, in the beginning was, / and nought without Him ever can be done'; Pulci, p. 3) strips the Word—reduced to an almost irreverent 'Him'—of all theological value, and says little more than 'without words one cannot talk'— and yet it is still the Word that is in question here. And it is the same with the prologue to *Pantagruel*, which enjoins the reader to believe in its chronicles 'like the text of the Bible or the Holy Gospel' if they do not wish to be consumed by Saint Anthony's fire or suffer from bloody stools (Rabelais, p. 11).

At issue is nothing less than the inscription of language (or at least its body) in a sort of antitheology, just as Pantagruel salutes the mount of the Muses as an Antiparnassus ('*les Muses de cestuy mons Antiparnasse*') with a peal of cannon fire (p. 867). The entire voyage of Pantagruel and his companions in the Fourth Book is not only 'buttressed' from the beginning 'by reflections [. . .] drawn from Holy Writ' but is punctuated here and there by explicit Biblical references ('That same day Pantagruel called at the two islands of Tohu

and Bohu, where we found we had no fish to fry'; pp. 666, 714). And the aforementioned genealogy of Pantagruel is undoubtedly theological—or rather, antitheological—which, as has been calculated, includes exactly the same number of generations that go from Adam to Christ (sixty-one, one less than the Biblical one, because Rabelais has them begin not at the time of Adam, but that of Cain and Abel).

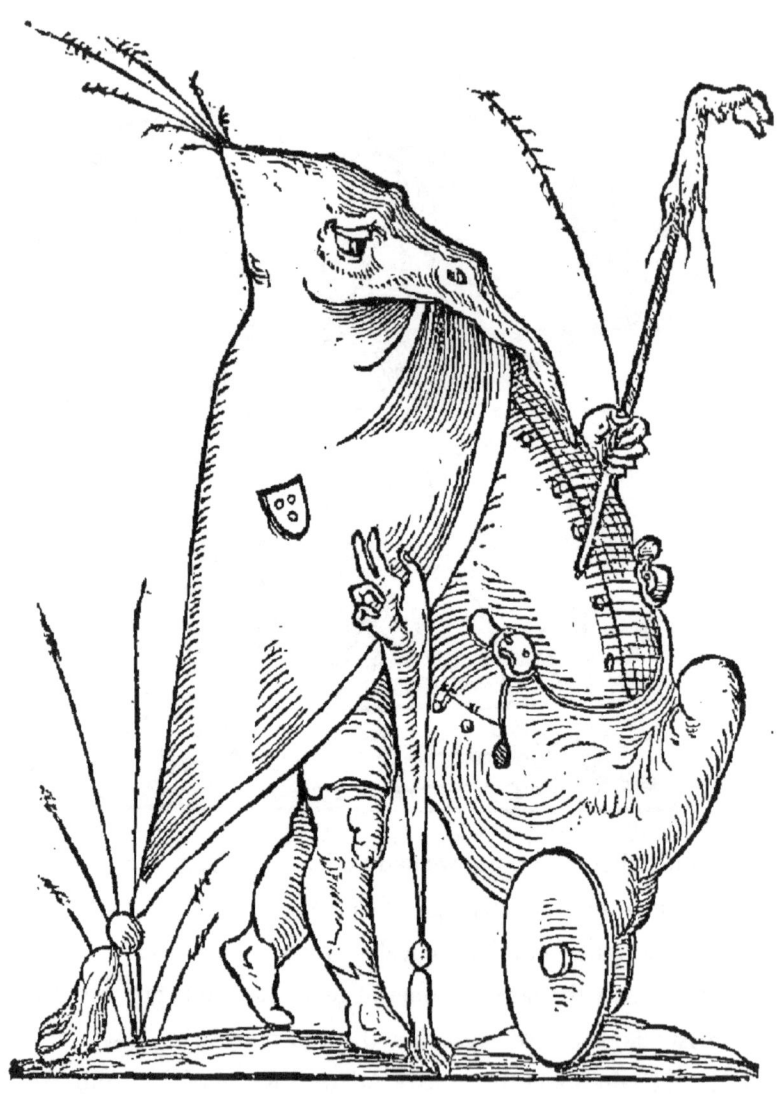

That is a significant fact because it implies, on the one hand, that Pantagruel is not, like Christ, a new Adam, and, on the other, that his genealogy has little to do with the sacred one and seems to run in some way autonomously parallel to it. The giants, in any case, do not descend from Adam and perhaps, anticipating the thesis of La Peyrère, bear witness to the stubborn survival of a pre-Adamic humanity. They originate from men who have eaten the fruits of the 'Year of the Fat Medlars', which provoke 'most horrible bulges, though not all in the same places' in the bodies of those who ingest them (pp. 16–17).

> In some it was their bellies that swelled up, and those bellies grew as convex as fat barrels. Of them it is written, *Almighty and Everlasting Guts*. [. . .] Others swelled up behind the shoulders, and were so hunchbacked that men called them *montiferi* (mountain-bearers, as it were). [. . .] Others swelled in length along that member which we call Nature's plough-share, so that theirs became marvellously long, big, plump fat, verdant and cockscombed in the antique style, so much so that they used them as girdles, wrapping them five or six times round their middles. (p. 17)

On some their bollocks swelled up, on others their legs, and on others their noses, so that 'they looked like the beaks of alembics: noses bespeckled and bespangled with papules'. Others, finally, 'grew in length of body. From them came the giants and, through them,

Pantagruel' (p. 18). The giants are not a race or a people: they are, rather, the fruit of a different, random bloating of bodies caused by indigestion.

The first name in the genealogy—Chalbroth—also contains a parodic allusion to the Bible, namely, to the giant Nembroth, who also figures in Pantagruel's genealogy and whom Genesis 10:9 describes as 'a mighty hunter before the Lord' (indeed, 'against the Lord', as the earliest Latin version of the Bible has it). It should be remembered that in the *Inferno*, Dante punished 'Nimrod' by having him speak an incomprehensible language ('*Raphel may amich zabí almí*'; 31.67), something that Rabelais could not have easily missed. The first three names on the genealogical list, which Rabelais entirely made up, all sound Hebrew: Chalbroth (from *chal*, he performed, he completed, and *broth*, covenant) can mean 'he who performs or completes the covenant or the law'; Sarabroth (from *sar*, to recede, to descend, and *broth*) can mean 'he who recedes from or moves away from the pact or the law'; Faribroth (from *fara*, he fructified) is perhaps he who has drawn fruit from the pact or law—but what pact or law this might refer to is impossible to determine—whether that between the Jews and Yahweh, or rather some pact among rogues and scoundrels. In any case, the most cunning giant neither fulfils nor breaks the law; rather, he knows how to make it bear fruit.

4. That language has a body, that the word has always already been made flesh, that it is first of all material and corporeal, is clearly shown by the extraordinary episode of the frozen words in the Fourth Book: 'At [the onset of last winter], the Words and cries of men and the women [. . .] froze in the air. And now that the rigour of winter has passed and fine, calm, temperate weather returned, they melt, and can be heard' (Rabelais, p. 829), at which point Pantagruel can grab some still-unthawed ones and throw fistfuls of them at his friends. The words—coloured azure, sable, golden—

> after they had been warmed up a little in our hands [. . .] melted like snow, and we actually heard them but did not understand them, for they were in some barbarous tongue, save for a rather tubby one which, after Frère Jean had warmed it in his hands, made a sound such as chestnuts make when they are tossed un-nicked on to the fire and go pop. (p. 829)

Beyond the imaginative invention, the frozen words are in some way the paradigm of the new Pantagruelian antilanguage—horrific and bloody and yet fully aware of its own dignity. When Panurge asks him for another fistful of words, the giant objects that 'Giving Words is what lovers do'; nor can they be sold, as his friend then requests, because 'selling Words is what lawyers do'; 'I would rather,' he immediately adds, 'sell you silence more dearly' (pp. 829–30).

In any case, what is at issue here is the unprecedented body of language, a body that lets itself be seen, bleeds and rumbles:

And I saw many sharp Words, and bloodthirsty Words too (which the pilot said come home to roost with the man that uttered them and cut his throat); there were dreadful Words,

and others unpleasant to behold. When they had all melted together we heard: *Hing, hing, hing, hing: hisse; hickory, dickory, dock; brededing, brededac, frr, frrr, frrr, bou, bou bou, bou, bou, bou, bou, bou. Ong, ong, ong, ong, ouououong; Gog, magog* and who-knows-what other barbarous words; and the pilot said that they were vocables from battles joined and from horses neighing at the moment of the charge; and then we heard other ones, fat ones which made sounds when they melted, some of drum or fife; others of bugle and trumpet. Believe you me, they provided us with some excellent sport.

I had hoped to preserve a few gullet-words in oil, wrapping them up in very clean straw (as we do with snow and ice); but Pantagruel would not allow it, saying that it was madness to pickle something which is never lacking and always to hand. (p. 830)

Language is not—contrary to a stale doctrine that the West tirelessly repeats—the sign of a mental concept: it is first of all a body that can be seen, heard and touched—a body that, like those of the giants, has its own physiology and its own anatomy, fingernails and heels, buttocks and belly, nerves and armpits. In any case, one does not understand the doctrine of Rabelais and Folengo, of Pantagruel and Baldo, of Cingar and Panurge, unless one resolutely places oneself at the point where the two bodies intersect.

5. The crossing of the two bodies produces what Folengo bluntly calls a *buffonus*, that is, a human exemplar *sui generis*, removed from both heavenly grace and the punishment of hell. When the rather sketchy brigade made up of the magisters Acquarius Lodola, Salvanellus Boccatorta, Dimeldeus Zucconus, Ioannes Baricocola and Buttadeus Gratarogna, and the four Jewish doctors Samuel, Nabaioth, Helcana and Ruch enters the dark cave below an enormous mountain—which in those who enter '*non pocam mentis cagarolam incutiebat*' (provoked not a little mental shitting; Folengo, *Le Maccheronee*, pp. 276–77)—they eventually arrive, *caminantes caminantes*, moving further and further down, before a sepulchre. The first thing they do is decipher an epitaph written with wine on an urn that looks rather like a cask:

> *Nec in coelo gratia nec in inferno poena datur*
> *bofonibus, hic ergo vivam Bocalus*

> Neither the grace of heaven nor the punishment of hell is granted
> to buffoons; here, therefore, shall I, Bocalus, live.

The character who emerges from it—*magrefactum barbatumque usque ad umbilicum* (gaunt and bearded down to his navel)—offers Folengo an opportunity for a sort of metaphysics of buffoonery. Asked to identify himself, he first responds with a speech that is *aenigmatizatum et dignum oedipodensci splanatione* [in the form of a

riddle and worthy of an Oedipus-like explanation]: 'I am he who I was, but will be he who I was not, if you will have given that which you did not give.' This theological head-scratcher is, in reality, nothing other than a definition of the buffoon, who immediately declines his unclassifiable generalities: 'It seems I am a buffoon, whom neither heaven nor hell can welcome' (p. 279). And what the nine magisters then find themselves contemplating and learning (*nec pochinum imparare* [but not learning much]) is that 'buffoon-men' (*homines buffones*) constitute a separate type, strangers to both heaven (grace) and hell (the law)—the two fundamental theological categories of the New Testament—and that in some way they deserve to be honoured, because 'in their buffoonery they take us away from our melancholies' (p. 279).

There has been much talk, and rightly so, about laughter in the universe of Rabelais and Folengo, laughter that borders on death, eating and excrement: but nothing about this laughter is truly understood if one does not see that its true place is language, that the entire physiological-anatomical universe that this laughter marks out is, first of all, speech, that phlegm like gnocchi, farts like sausages, diarrhoea like must and beer are nothing other than the movements—awkward, but in their way disciplined—of an unprecedented and unassignable language—a language fleeing towards who knows where, but certainly beyond all grammatical identity and any defined lexicon.

6. That Folengo is much more than the 'pinnacle of the *ars macaronica*'—that is, more than just a relatively minor poet, even if he 'far surpasses all of his macaronic predecessors in both expertise and versification'—is clear from the *Chaos del triperuno* (*Chaos of the Triperuno*), a work which has been overshadowed by the exuberance

of his macaronic poems. But before being 'one of the most tangled messes of our literature' (Folena, p. 147), it is perhaps the most complex and acrobatic invention in all of sixteenth-century Italian literature. Not only is the book, written in alternating prose and verse, composed in three languages (the vernacular, Latin and macaronic), but Folengo, with unusual audacity, splits himself into three heteronyms ('we are of three names: Merlino, Limerno, Fùlica'; Folengo, *Chaos*, p. 14), who come together in Triperuno (three-for-one), who is none other than Folengo himself. The whole book is based 'for an appropriate reason' (p. 13) on the third:

> First you see that the title of the book is in three words: *Chaos del triperuno*. Then the three black birds [*folenghe*] follow, or rather they are called merles [*fòliche*], which are the ancient coat of arms of our House in Mantua. And under their auspices follow the three women of three different ages and three different types of kinship, from whom the three prolix arguments are derived, each one being divided into three parts. (p. 14)

The *Chaos*, then, is divided into three forests and contains the life of the author, 'which up until this present hour with the time has swiftly passed by in three phases' (p. 7). It is, therefore, an autobiography, but this autobiography, with an explicit allusion to the *Commedia*, is also a voyage of initiation and a 'beautiful allegory' (p. 6), as it is described in the opening dialogue of the poem by Livia, niece of the poet, speaking to Corona, Folengo's sister (the allegorical suggestion is furthermore supported by the great number of enigmatic acrostics scattered throughout the text). A truly peculiar dialogue, as the three women who take part in it—with an invention that is certainly not banal—not only discuss the very author who makes them speak, but also propose three different interpretations of the text. No less peculiar is that in a lengthy macaronic *excursus*, Merlin writes a summary of the *Baldo*, which not only introduces some new elements into it, but places the macaronic under the authoritative invocation of Virgil—that is to say, of the greatest representative of Latin poetry. An exemplary moment is the opening, which parodically cites the spurious *incipit* of Virgil:

> *Ille ego qui quondam formaio plenus et ovis,*
> *quique, botirivoro stipans ventrone lasagnas,*
> *arma valenthominis cantavi horrencia Baldi,*
> *quo non Hectorior, quo non Orlandior alter,*
> *grandisonam cuius phanam nomenque gaiardum*
> *terra tremit baratrumque metu se cagat adossum,*
> *at nunc Tortelii egressus gymnasia, postquam*
> *tanta menestrarum smaltita est copia, Baldi*
> *gesta maronisono cantemus digna stivallo.*

> I am he who, once upon a time full of cheese and eggs, and who, packing lasagna into my butter-gorging belly, sang about the terrifying force of that knight Baldo,

of whom no one is more Hector-like or more Roland-like.
His resounding frame and brave name
shake the earth and [make] the underworld beshit itself in fear.
But now having left the college of Tortelli, after
such an abundance of minestrone has been digested, let us
sing deeds worthy of a Maro-styled boot. (p. 72)

The linguistic *chaos* of the *Triperuno* is in reality yet another unconditional declaration of the dignity of his beloved macaronic creature. The fact remains that, as Momigliano noted, 'in its century the *Baldo* did not find even one noble critic who deigned to give it a serious examination' and that the work was condemned in the Clementine *Index* of 1596 (Momigliano, p. 177). No less significant, however, is the fact that Folengo's work did not escape the notice of Giordano Bruno, who evokes Mafelina Lodola—the macaronic muse of astronomy, particularly dear to Folengo—in the London katabasis of the *Ash Wednesday Supper*.

7. What is macaronic? So far, we have spoken of it as a 'language', though Folengo defines it rather as a 'fat-oloquy' (*meum hoc grassiloquium*), a *genus parlandi* (type of speech) or a *parlatio* (speech) (*Le Maccheronee*, p. 284). But are we really dealing with a language? The question hinges not only on the fact that, as has been observed, there exist as many different macaronics as there are authors who write them (*Migliorini*, p. 7); the crucial point is that there is not *one* language, but a complicated, hybrid mixture between *two* languages, which seems to call into question, above all, what we usually consider the identity of a language: that is, that Italian is not French, Latin is not Greek, Turkish is not Chinese.

'By "macaronic", a linguist has written,

> we mean an artificial language that consists in the parodic Latinization of words and phrases in dialect, or the deformation in dialect of Latin words; the interweaving between Latin and the vernacular varies widely among writers, with the greatest "expressionistic" tension (that is, the greatest "dramatization" of the linguistic extremes) between the two components forced to blend with each other: on the one hand the lower, strongly rustic stratum of the vernacular [. . .] which provides the greater part of the lexical material, and on the other, Latin, which in most cases provides the grammatical structure. (Tavoni, p. 159)

But whether this 'artificial language' is truly a language and not a jargon or *Sabir* is anything but a settled question.

In 1909, Hugo Schuchardt, one of the leaders of the school of linguists known as the neogrammarians, decided to publish a study on the 'lingua franca', which—as he himself tells us—he no longer hoped to bring to a successful conclusion. The lingua franca (from the Arabic *lisan al-farand*) is that curious amalgam of primarily Italian and Spanish terms used by coastal populations (Arabs, Italians, Spaniards, Levantines) to communicate with each other in the ports of the southeast Mediterranean. Perhaps the most interesting moment of Schuchardt's essay is precisely where the linguist—faced with phrases like *en Berberia fezer forte agua Cielo* (In Barbary heavy rain fell from the sky) or *mi poudir servir per ti per qualké cosa?* (How can I help you?)—wonders in bewilderment if we have before us an autonomous language or merely the pure and simple mangling (*Radebrechen*) of one or more preexisting languages. Depending on whether we move westward or the eastward in the Mediterranean, a Spanish or Italian coloration will prevail in the idiom, yet, what always remains fixed is the absence of any definable grammar. Thus, the lingua franca comes to occupy a zone of indifference and non-identity that our grammatical conception of language is utterly unable to define. The result is a language with no certified designation of origin, as Amedeo Giacomini would say of himself and his dialect.

Indeed, every language is characterized by a grammar, that is, the principle by which the differential opposition 'one says / one does not say', 'acceptable form / unacceptable form' holds true, even if law and fact do not always align and it is not always easy to distinguish between errors and variants of usage. Lingua franca, jargon, like Folengo's macaronic, disrupt precisely this fundamental opposition on which every grammar rests: indeed, in them one says exactly what one cannot say, what is acceptable is precisely unacceptable, in such a way that not only does the boundary between bad usage and good usage disappear and lose all meaning, but good usage coincides exactly with incorrectness. There is indeed no doubt that the writer of macaronic mangles and misuses Latin no less than the vernacular.

Is a language that solely consists in the misuse of another language a new language—or simply a mangled one? Despite the parodic *normula* that concludes the Toscolanese edition, this is the undecidable dilemma that jargons and macaronics pose to the linguist.

8. If the impossibility of a grammatical definition is something that *Sabir* and macaronic have in common, it is an entirely different case when it comes to the function they serve. While the lingua franca was born in the ports of the Mediterranean from the need—essentially pragmatic and commercial—for mutual understanding among alloglots, macaronic belongs to an eminently literary milieu and is addressed to people who understand both mixed languages with ease. In order to understand its meaning, we must therefore begin by restoring it to its context, which is not the language question (as we would say today) but the question of languages, as suggested by the title of the dialogue by Sperone Speroni (1542), and in particular the question of Latin's or the vernacular's primacy, which so intensely occupied the Venetian and Florentine scholars of that time. Bembo's *Prose della volgar lingua* (*Discussions of the Vernacular Language*), though begun years earlier, appears in 1525, between the Toscolanense and Cipadense editions of *Baldo*. The canonization of Petrarch and Boccaccio's fourteenth-century Tuscan could not have but displeased Folengo, who puts in the mouth of one of his heteronyms, Limerno, the naive arguments of Bembo in defence of 'Tosco':

> Above all the others, I deem that language worthy, I praise, exalt and defend it vigorously against all its detractors; because when under these shades I find that I have in hand the poetry of my Francesco Petrarca, or that fountain of eloquence, Boccaccio, I lose myself in them, and I become a

> stone, a log, a phantasm, due to excessive amazement at so much learning. What more elegant verse, polished, full and sonorous than that of Petrarca can one read? What prose oration can one compare in learning, in art, in wit, in propriety, to that of the most eloquent Boccaccio? For this reason, I deem literary men who take no delight in this language to be devoid, not just of [the language], but of gentility, kindness and humanity. (Folengo, *Chaos*, pp. 96–97)

'Ah, pig's snout and gallows bird that you are', Merlin replies insolently, marvelling at

> other ignoramuses like you, who, not understanding one iota of Ciceronian eloquence or Virgilian gravity, have completely fixated on and gotten seduced by 'hither and thither', 'just now', 'likewise', 'whoever', 'not as yet', 'nonetheless' and other vocabulary used by a Tuscan. (p. 97)

It goes without saying that in noting the 'Ciceronian eloquence and Virgilian gravity', Folengo had no intention of taking the side of Latin, which he has no qualms about scrambling and mangling. What seemed to him unacceptable in the Bembian canon was not so much the choice of the vernacular as it was the peremptory affirmation of 'Petrarchan unilingualism' (as Contini calls it) against Dante's plurilingualism and plurality of tones and lexical layers. He could not possibly have approved of the pedantic, courtly exclusion of the *Commedia* from the canon, which Bembo compares to a lovely and wide field of grain, all covered in oats or rye mixed with fruitless and harmful grasses, or to some vines that are left unpruned which one sees later in the summer so full of foliage and vine leaves and tendrils, and which are an offence to the fine grapes. (Bembo, p. 178)

The conception of language that Folengo develops—indeed, the conception of the bodily *parlatio* that cannot be separated from the mind—suggests that he had no claim to place himself among Giuliano de' Medici, messer Ercole Strozza, Federigo Fregoso, and the others with whom Bembo pretends to converse 'in Vinegia' (Venice).

9. The first edition of the *Baldo* is Venetian: *Venetiis in aedibus Alexandri Paganini, inclito Lauredano principe, kal. ian. MDXVII.* And to restore it to its context, it will be quite helpful to compare it to another famous book published in Venice exactly eighteen years earlier: the *Hypnerotomachia Poliphili*. At first glance, nothing could appear further from Folengo's coarse irreverence than this precious, esoteric incunabulum with its enigmatic illustrations. And yet, one need only pay a little attention to the language in which Polifilo's dream is transcribed to realize that we find ourselves in the same linguistic fabric, albeit somewhat inverted (and we can see a certain proximity also in the attention with which Folengo chose his illustrations, which unfortunately are not reproduced in modern editions). As Leonardo Crasso's dedicatory epistle in Latin clearly states,

what is marvellous about the book is that although it is written in the vernacular (*cum nostrati lingua loquatur*), Latin is no less necessary for understanding it than 'Tuscan and the vernacular'. The operation that the monk in love with Polia carries out on language is exactly the inverse of what macaronic does: just as Folengo implacably Latinizes the vernacular, no less stubbornly does Francesco Colonna vernacularize Latin. In the words of a scholar who has dedicated exemplary attention to the *Hypnerotomachia*, the incunabulum is 'an attempt to resolve with a practical formula the humanistic quarrel between the vernacular and Latin, preserving the phonetic and morphological reality of the former and the lexical nobility of the latter' (Colonna, p. 79). If the macaronic idiom starts with the vernacular and invents terms that seem Latin but exist in neither Latin nor any other language (*bisognat, bagordum, sbadacchiant, se cagat addossum*), the author of the *Hypnerotomachia*—whether his name is Francesco Colonna or not—begins with Latin stems and suffixes and forges countless vernacular neologisms that are morphologically possible, yet never before seen (*illachrymando, latibuli, obliquiescente, somnoso, siccitutudine, caverniculato, nympheaticamente, cypiri, pavore, siticoloso, irascibondo, undiculare, simulabondo, tenebrifico, haesitamento, smaragdineo* ...). Hence, the impression of slowness, almost of a *ritardando*, as if the vernacular were struggling to carry within itself the heavy, opaque Latin lemmas—just as, conversely, in the *Baldo*, the vernacular inserts produce an effect of *accelerando* in the Latin context. This is, to evoke Giovanni Pozzi's formula, a case of two symmetrically opposed efforts, both certainly parodic even if differently oriented, to resolve 'the humanistic quarrel between the vernacular and Latin'. As long as we clarify that what the two monks aim at is not so much a resolution, but rather the tenacious, lengthy exhibition of an irreducible diglossia, a split within the body of language for which no conciliation seems possible.

10. What does it mean to give a body to language? In 1910, the young Leo Spitzer published his dissertation *Die Wortbildung als stilistisches Mittel exemplifiziert an Rabelais* (Word-formation as a stylistic device exemplified by Rabelais). Beginning with an analysis of Meringer's and Freud's linguistic errors, Spitzer precisely reconstructs how the formation of non-existent words happens unconsciously: the switching of suffixes, the anticipation of the subsequent word, the echo and contamination of one word with another. Closest to his heart, though, is the formation intentionally sought by an author for a comic stylistic effect. His catalogue of spontaneous coinages in Rabelais records formations that are farcical (*chacun s'en va à sa chascunière*, 'off they went, every man to his manor'; Rabelais, p. 79), decidedly burlesque (*Condieux*, 'fellow gods', from *concitoyens*), and grotesque (*Sorbillans, Sorbonagres, Sorbonigenes, Sorbonucoles, Sorboniformes, Sorbonisecques, Saniborsans* . . . to mock the tribe of scholastics of the Sorbonne), as well as the accumulation of synonyms (*cagotz, caffars, botineurs, porteurs de rogatons, abbreviateurs, scripteurs, copistes, Bulistes, Dataires, Chiquaneurs, caputons . . . Sanctorons, Patepellues,*

Torticollis, Dominotiers, Maminotiers, Paternostriers . . .). The accumulation of synonyms and paronyms gives rise to a tendency for endless lists, which will leave a long legacy in baroque prose writers, from Giordano Bruno and Bartoli up to Jarry and Manganelli. Here, words germinate one from the other, transforming the entire lexicon into an endless, senseless pseudosynonymy: '*Couillons d'alidada, d'algamala, d'algebra . . . couillons magistral, claustral, monachal . . . madré, relevé, de stuc . . . fulminant, tonnant, estincelant, couillons de crotesque, Arabesque, asseré, troussé à la levresque, masculinant, ronssinant'* (alidadic bollock, amalgamic b., algebraic b. . . . don's b. claustral b., monkish b. . . . doctor-hooded b., well-seasoned b., stucco'd b. . . . fulminating b., thundering b., glistening b., grotesque b., arabesque b., steel-braced b., trussed-hare b., masculinizing b., stallionizing b.) (Spitzer, pp. 115–16; Rabelais,

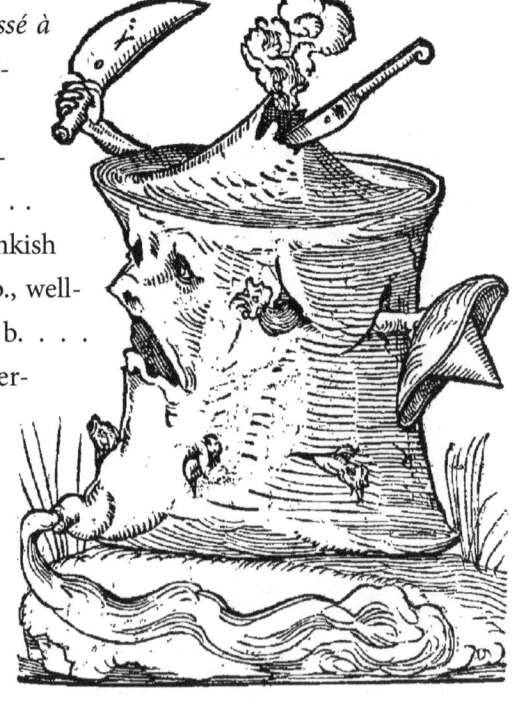

pp. 510–11). The inventory of the internal and external organs of Quarêmeprenant's body, each one incongruously likened to an object that has nothing to do with it ('a brain which ... is like the left testicle of a male tick'; Rabelais, p. 752), takes up several pages. The catalogue can at times be reinforced by an inflectional rhyme, with the supposed synonymy emphasized to the point of being lost in absurdity (*Puis fianoit, pissoyt, rendoyt sa gorge, rottoit, pettoyt, baisloyt, crachoyt, touissoyt, sangluoyt, esternouit, et se morvoyt en archidiacre*; 'He would then shit, piss, hawk, fart, break wind, yawn, gob, cough, snivel, sneeze and dribble snot like an archdeacon'; Spitzer, p. 117; Rabelais, p. 269). As Bakhtin noted, this is an example of a taste for seriality, in this case excremental. Seriality can at times be purely sonorous, without any semantic claims, as in: *toujours apprendre, fust ce / d'un sot, d'un pot, d'une guedoufle / d'une moufle, d'une pantoufle*, 'always learning something, even from a sot, a pot, a mug, a kitten or a mitten' (Rabelais, p. 471). In one of the rare Italian writers of Folengo's time who refer to him, Anton Francesco Doni, whose lineage from the poet has been rightly acknowledged (Rodda, p. 186), the macaronic taste for gratuitous enumeration reaches Rabelasian tones:

> You are the prideful ones, the simpletons, the pedants, the lickspittles, the saps who quibble over everything. I would not grant you one iota, you pack of tiresome, unhinged, insipid fools, you heap of bric-a-brac, who have only unleashed a spawn of raving, vaporous, scrawny, confused, flyaway words. (Doni, p. 474)

11. In all these cases, what changes is not so much the syntax but the lexicon, not the grammatical structure but, so to speak, the body parts of the language. Not the rules governing the dynamic structure of propositions but rather the static, antidynamic element of the language: the plane of terms, which thus acquires an unusual movement. The neoformations create a new body for the marionette of language, independent of the strings that move it. But how far can a term be transformed and still retain its meaning? To be sure, the language of the poets is always marked by a tension towards terminological invention; but what in the poets remains an impulse—usually directed at already-existing words, to which they restore their original naming power—intensifies, in Rabelais, in Folengo and in their descendants, into unrestrained coinage and onomastic transgression. All—or nearly all—words become neologisms (as Bakhtin said: all names become nicknames). At the extreme end of this we have Nina Cassian's Spargan ('Your multikunk entankler, your dimical so phlooger, / And cloff on many flanches, on spinch, on sminch, on swack'; Cassian, p. 68) and the *fanfole* of Fosco Maraini ('*Il lonfo non vaterca né gluisce / e molto raramente barigatta, / ma quando soffia il bego a bisce bisce / sdilenca un poco, e gnagio s'archipatta*').

The adulteration of the semiotic leads to an abolition of the semantic, and both tear up and invalidate the identity card of any language. Is Rabelais's language still French, Folengo's still vernacular or Latin? The new words jostle in the interstices between existing ones,

tracing the contours of a language that exists only at the edges of attested languages. Here we must apply to languages the theorem Shlomo Pines formulated for cultures (in particular, Judaism): just as the identity of a culture is not a given but a problem, and the only certain fact is its changing historical trajectory, which, as in the case of Judaism, appears rather as a sort of lacework on the borders of other cultures and languages, so too the identity of a language is something essentially problematic, which, in its historical unfolding, incessantly spills out beyond itself. While the humanists were rediscovering the true identity of Latin, which, precisely for this reason, appeared for the first time as a dead language in contrast with the vernacular (something it had never been until Dante and Petrarch), Folengo revives it by unscrupulously hybridizing it with the vernacular, which for its part gets counterfeited and crushed into a pseudo-Latin. The *tertium* between the two languages—macaronic—is not properly a language—it is a dumpling, not to be spoken, but chewed and swallowed. In any case, it is something corporeal, indeed corpulent and excessive, like the body of the giants.

12. In his letter to Henry More on 5 February 1649, Descartes at one point claims that he is not in the habit of arguing about words (*ego vero non soleo quidem de nominibus disputari*). This phrase, which philosophers will repeat many times, in turn recalls an affirmation by Galen, who, in a text that has had a notable influence on the history of thought, the *De Hippocratis et Platonis decretiis*, wrote that because we use words to express concepts that reflect the nature of things, 'it is foolish, neglecting the concepts, to argue about words (*peri tōn onomatōn homilasthai*)'.

The truth of this affirmation, which on first glance seems obvious, requires a few caveats. When we speak and listen, and even when we read, the materiality of sound and the patina it burnishes on every word fade so little into conceptual meaning and denotation that we can say the world reveals itself differently each time, according to the particularities and nature of the words and the style of the speaker or writer. It is true that a centuries-long scholastic and academic tradition has habituated us to distinguish between poetic-literary discourse and philosophical-scientific discourse, and to confine attention to colour, rhythm and tone of expression to the former. But it is sufficient to recall how the elegance and vivacity of Galileo's writing speaks to us in such a different way than does Newton's prose, and how Spinoza's Latin, even though it was thought of as a neutral language of communication among the learned, could never be confused with that of the *Regulae* of Descartes's letters, to realize that even in science and philosophy meanings are in no way separable from their signifiers. Not only the poet and the literary writer, but also the philosopher and the scientist must dwell on words: *necesse est de nominibus disputari*.

13. Melanchthon must have had something like this in mind when he wrote in the 'Praise of Eloquence':

> In shaping bodies there is elegance only when all the members agree among themselves in the right proportion, and, if you make anything otherwise, it becomes monstrous. In just the same way, if you spoil the genuine form of a speech by a new arrangement you make it simply monstrous and silly

(*monstruosam atque ineptam*). [...] Does the painter imitate the body correctly if he guides his brush without any method, and if his hand is moved at random and the lines are not drawn with art? In the same way you will not put the sentiment of your mind in front of the others' eyes unless you use appropriate and distinct words (*propriis et illustribus verbis*), a fitting arrangement of words and the right order of sentences. For, just as we represent bodies by colours, we represent the sentiment of our mind by speech (*animi sententiam oratione repraesentamur*). Therefore it is necessary for one who speaks to conceive a certain image (*certam aliquam imaginem*) through art, which marks out the faces—so to speak—of the sentences against each other (*quae discernat inter se tanquam vultus sententiarum*). (Melanchthon, p. 63).

The idea that meanings have a face calls into question the interpretation of language that Aristotle had put forth in *On Interpretation*. While for Aristotle words were signs (*sēmeia*) or symbols (*sumbola*) of the affections of the soul, and these in turn likenesses or images (*homoiōma*) of things, now it is the words themselves that are defined as images, or even paintings, of meanings. In other words, meanings have a face, made up of luminous and well-ordered words, like a portrait. And just as any face can be caricatured, making it, as Melanchthon warned, 'monstrous and silly', the extemporaneous formations of Rabelais and the *menchionica verba* of Folengo are caricatures transposed into the realm of language. The flourishing of 'burlesque, or rather, caricatured portraits', as Bellori defined them in reference to the Carraccis, happens at more or less the same time (even if their origin can be traced to Leonardo's caricatures). And just as caricatures, if they truly are such, resemble the original too closely ('with ridiculous resemblance', Bellori said), so the neoformations of Pantagruel and Baldo exaggerate the 'face of meaning' to the

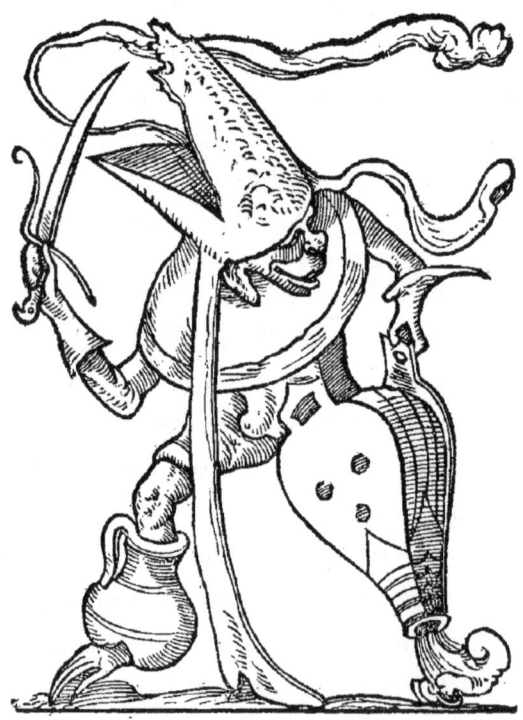

point where we can no longer recognize it. In both cases, the laughter they provoke mocks the identity of each of the two bodies—the body of language no less that the body of flesh and blood.

14. In his treatise on translation (*De interpretatione recta*), Leonardo Bruni argues that the perfect translation is the one that transfers into another language not only the meaning of words but also their sensory element—their splendour and beauty (*nitor ornatusque*). Like a painter copying someone else's painting, the translator must be able to express 'the figure, the status, the gait, the colour and the lineaments of the discourse (*orationis figuram, statum, ingressum coloremque et lineamenta cuncta*)'. It is possible to think of the neoformations of Folengo and Rabelais as translations not from one language into another but from one language into itself—that is, an operation on language that intensifies and pushes to an extreme 'the colour and the lineaments' that belong to it. *Se cagat addossum* would therefore not be an incorrect translation of the vernacular into Latin, but rather a forcing of the vernacular words against themselves, which, through a morphological alteration, produces an intensification of meaning (*se cagat addossum* is more than simply 'he beshits himself'). The same can be said of the 'portmanteau words' (as Humpty Dumpty calls them) in Rabelais: six French (or slang) words glued together exaggerate the meaning they aim to express, shifting (trans-lating) it into a language that is neither another nor itself, which in its extreme form Rabelais calls *barragouyn*. When Panurge

meets Pantagruel and his companions, he immediately translates what he has to say in German, Dutch, Hebrew, Italian, Gaelic, etc. and finally bursts out in a *barragouyn*, which Epistemon defines as the 'language of the Antipodes, I think. The devil himself couldn't sink his teeth into it . . . ' (Rabelais, p. 52). Rabelais's entire work, in this sense, is written in a *barragouyn*—a term that, according to the aforementioned *Etymologisches Wörterbuch*, likely derives not from the Italian *baraonda* (confusion, chaos) but from the Breton *bara gwin*, bread and wine. Bread and wine—this is not just a matter of finding a language for the body; rather, it is about inventing another body of language.

15. The body of the giant is made of words, and, vice versa, his language is something eminently corporeal. The first consequence of this irrefutable entwining of body and language is that Pantagruel's and Margutte's mass lies not in a neutral geometric space but in a vernacular *locus* that the giants, when they move, shift and carry with them. In Rabelais's antitheology it is not the Word that is *apud Deum* but God that is *apud Verbum*, in its immense speaking body, made of hyperboles and paronyms, quarrels and idiotisms, epanalepses and barbarisms. This is why the author, lost in the five kingdoms of Pantagruel's mouth, does not observe, as we might expect, that 'one half of the world has no idea *where* the other half lives' but rather that it 'has no idea *how* the other half lives'. For the giant, space is not a 'where' but a 'how', not a place where the body is found

but its very corpulence, its features, and its exuberant visibility, which all move along with him. The meticulous anatomy of Qarêmeprenant, in which every organ and every part of the body is displaced outside of itself and offered to the gaze as an improbable implement, is in this sense paradigmatic. The anatomy of the giant is, in truth, a physiognomy. A body that is pure expressivity and surfaces is not *in* a space; it *is* spacious: spaciousness in motion that coincides with its unruly physiognomy.

Chapter Two

The Body of the Philosophers

1. The political thought of the baroque period is a thought of the body. It seeks to define, organize, discipline, measure, control—in a word, politicize and govern—bodies. Its first task is therefore a philosophy of the body that defines its characteristics and situates it in the world. In 1654, Hobbes's *De corpore* (more precisely: *Elementorum philosophiae sectio prima DE CORPORE*) was published by Andrew Crooke (note the last name) in London. His *De corpore politico* had appeared, as the second part of the *Elements of Law*, fourteen years earlier and was dedicated to an investigation of 'how a multitude of persons natural are united by covenants into one person civil or body politic' (*Elements*, p. 109). For Hobbes, the physical body coincides with its extension in space: '*Corpus* is anything that, independently of our thought, coincides or is coextensive with a certain part of space (*cum spatii parte aliqua coincidit vel coextenditur*)'

(*De corpore*, p. 83). But if the definition of the body presupposes that of space, this is precisely where things get complicated. Indeed, for Hobbes, space is 'something imaginary' and a 'mere phantasm', and the body, which we call *suppositum* or *subiectum* because it 'seems to extend and lie under the imaginary space', coincides and is coextensive with something that does not exist. Indeed, space is that which we imagine when we remove a body from its place:

> If we remember or have a phantasm of something that existed before we think of it as removed and we do not want to consider how that thing was, but simply that it was outside of our mind, we then have what we call space, which is imaginary, since it is a mere phantasm (*imaginarium quidem, quia merum phantasma*), which is nevertheless that which everyone calls by this name. Indeed, no one calls it space when it is occupied, but only insofar as it can be occupied; and no one thinks that bodies carry their own places with them (*corpora loca sua secum absportare*), but that one body, then another body, is contained in the same space, which would not be possible if the space always accompanied the body that at one time was in it. (De corpore, p. 76).

Scholars have asked—and never fully answered—where Hobbes got the idea of imaginary space; yet in the fourteenth-century debates among philosophers and theologians about the problem of the void, the expression 'imaginary space' recurs a number of times, especially in the work of a writer, Thomas Bradwardine, that Hobbes could have known, given that it had been reprinted in London in 1618 by Henry Savile, a mathematician and astronomer at the University of Oxford. According to Bradwardine, the void is an imaginary space (*situs immaginarius*) that existed before the world and in which God is present at all times. From this—as stated in the corollary of the fifth chapter of the first book of his treatise *De causa Dei*—it follows that

> God is essentially and presentially everywhere, not only in the world and its parts, but also outside of the world in the infinite imaginary void or space (*extra mundum in situ seu vacuo imaginario infinito*). (Koyré, pp. 74–75)

Space is defined as 'imaginary' because 'it does not have any positive nature, otherwise there would be a positive nature that would not be God or from God' (Koyré, p. 78). That is to say, infinite empty space is something that must necessarily be imaginary because 'if there were not such a space not occupied by a body (*situs imaginarius corpore non repletus*), the world would be eternal, which is heretical' (Koyré, p. 78; More will say that we cannot 'disimagine space').

We can thus better understand Hobbes's peremptory gesture: he takes the definition of imaginary space out of its theological context and, erasing all divine presence from it, makes it the convenient, neutral presupposition to his ontology. 'Space,' his definition goes, 'is the phantasm of an existent thing as existent (*phantasma rei existentis quatenus existentis*)' (*De corpore*, pp. 76–77). The body that occupies this imaginary space is the pure existent: 'The being (*ens*) and the body (*corpus*) are the same thing' (Hobbes, *Critique*, p. 312) and the body is *id omne quod occupat spatium*. Imaginary space is therefore the phantasmatic apparatus that ultimately allows us to think being and body as pure extension.

2. If imaginary space is a phantasm without body, the extension of the body is, in fact, space made real: 'The extension of the body is the same thing as its size (*magnitudo*), or what some call *real space* (*spatium reale*)' (Hobbes, *De corpore*, p. 84). When imaginary space coincides with the size of a certain body, then it is called the place of the body (*corporis vocatur Locus*; *De corpore*, p. 85). But even place is a sort of phantasm, which must not be confused with size; it is an *extensio ficta*, while size is an *extensio vera*. What fascinates the mind of Hobbes and lies at the base of his corporeal ontology is extension, the fact that a body occupies a certain space and thus transforms the phantasm into a reality. If being and body are one, then being is nothing other than extension, the fact that a body always has a certain *magnitudo* and extends in all possible directions.

In the state of nature, the size of each body corresponds to its 'naturall Power', which is nothing other than 'the eminence of the Faculties of Body, or Mind: as extraordinary Strength, Forme, Prudence, Arts . . . ' (Hobbes, *Leviathan*, p. 62). This natural power translates into the 'Right of Nature', that is, into

> the Liberty each man hath, to use his own power, as he will himselfe, for the preservation of his own Nature; that is to say, of his own Life; and consequently, of doing any thing, which in his own Judgement, and Reason, hee shall conceive to be the aptest means thereunto. (*Leviathan*, p. 91)

The body from which Hobbes begins is, therefore, the same immense body of the giants, with their 'extraordinary Strength' and their natural claim over anything and everything that satisfies their immoderate appetite. And this premise is the basis of that 'restraint upon themselves' from which alone a 'Common-Wealth' can be born (*Leviathan*, p. 117).

3. The fascination (in the etymological sense of enchantment) that extension will continue to exert on the mind is evident in Descartes. Like Hobbes, he, too, thinks about the body, but the body is nothing but a synonym for extension, and extension in turn a synonym for space. In the *Principles of Philosophy*, the ontology founded upon this synonymy is outlined without reservation. In his usual gesture, Descartes calls into question the fundamental concept of scholastic ontology—substance (which is a translation of Aristotle's *ousia*)—reducing it simply to extension, that is, to show that 'if corporeal substance is distinguished from its quantity, it is conceived in a confused manner as something incorporeal' (Descartes, p. 226). He argues that we think of the nature of an extended thing that occupies the space of ten feet without attending to this measurement, but in truth 'there is no real difference between quantity and the extended substance; the difference is merely a conceptual one, like that between number and the thing which is numbered' (p. 226). It is evident that, if we remove a part of this extension, we also remove the thing, and if we remove the thing, we also remove the extension. The same goes for space.

> There is no real distinction between space [. . .] and the corporeal substance contained in it; the only difference lies in the way in which we are accustomed to conceive of them. For in reality the extension in length, breadth and depth which constitutes a space is exactly the same as that which constitutes a body. The difference arises as follows: in the case of a body, we regard the extension as something particular, and thus think of it as changing whenever there is a new body; but in the case of a space, we attribute to the extension only a generic unity, so that when a new body comes to occupy the space, the extension of the space is reckoned not to change but to remain one and the same, so long as it retains the same size and shape and keeps the same position relative to certain external bodies which we use to determine the space in question. (p. 227).

At this point, the identity of body and space by way of extension can be stated as a theorem: 'the extension constituting the nature of a body is exactly the same as that constituting the nature of a space' (p. 227). Indeed, if we remove from a body all its qualities (hardness, colour, heat, etc.), nothing remains 'except that it is something extended in length, breadth and depth. Yet this is just what is comprised in the idea of a space—not merely a space which is full of bodies, but even a space which is called "empty"' (pp. 227–28).

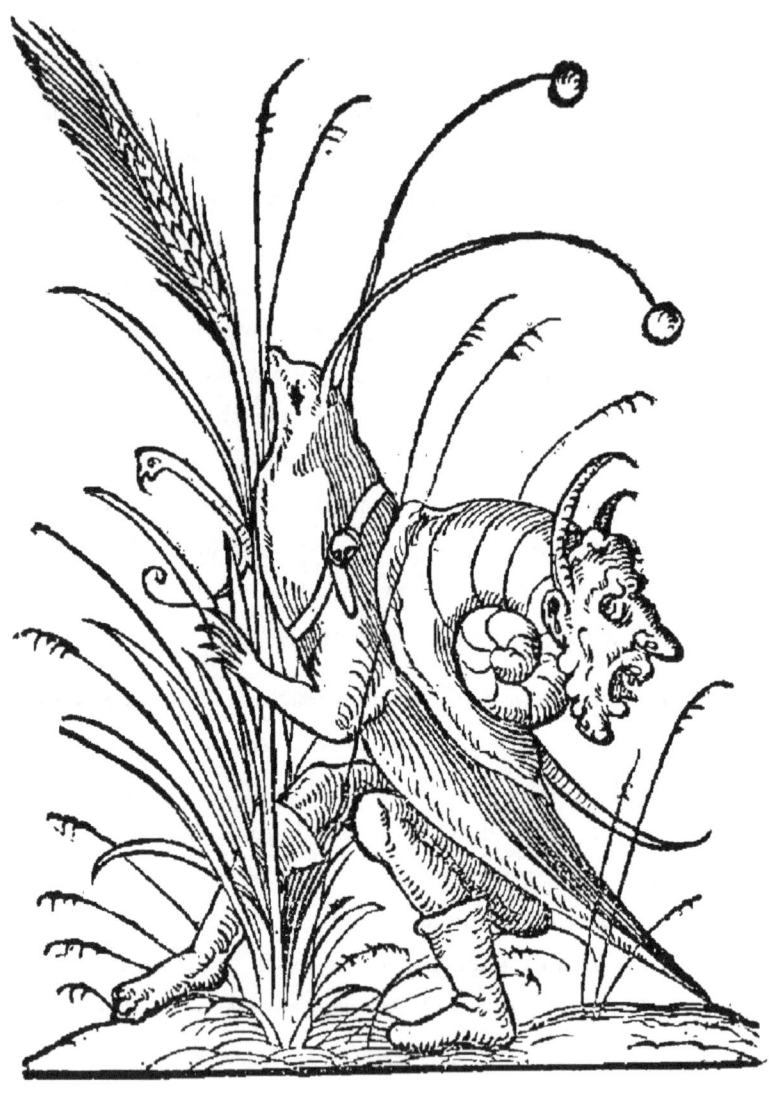

4. What is a body reduced to its extension? In the French translation of the *Principia*, next to *extension*—in which we can still hear an echo of *tonos*, the tension that, according to the stoics, animates matter—appears the term *estenduë*, the 'expanse' or 'stretch', the mere fact that a body occupies space, and it is this term that Descartes will use in his treatise *The World*. A body thus conceived does not differ at all from its dimensions, if it is true that 'there is no real difference between quantity and the extended substance; the difference is merely a conceptual one, like that between number and the thing numbered' (p. 226). In this way, the body of the giants is metaphysically disciplined far more than Hobbes sought to do politically through its inclusion in a Common-Wealth. If every body coincides with its measurements, bodies can be as big as one likes, but they will never be 'immense'. For Descartes, an empty space does not exist; there is always and only a space occupied by a body, always and only extension. Any and every body, no matter how alive and animated, can ultimately be reduced to the space it occupies in length, breadth and depth. This is the concept of the body that provides, so to speak, the metaphysical foundation for the space of analytic geometry, in which every point is defined by the three coordinates x, y and z. And it is no surprise that the *Discourse on the Method*—insofar as it was conceived, as reads the title of the first edition, for *rightly conducting one's reason and seeking the truth in the sciences*—concludes with a treatment of optics, meteorology and geometry, *qui sont les essais de cette Methode* (which are essays in this Method). The little human

head in a camera obscura or the bearded face that seems to look at the back of the retina in the illustrations of the *Optics* have nothing to do with the bodies of Rabelais and Folengo: they are nothing but the 'object ABC' which, passing through hole D of the camera obscura, is inverted into the 'image EFG' or the body at point P 'that casts its gaze on the white body RST'.

5. In *The World*, Descartes calls extension *matter*. By this term, he does not mean 'the "prime matter" of the philosophers, which they have stripped so thoroughly of all its forms and qualities that nothing remains in it which can be clearly understood'. Not that he, for his part, does not propose to consider it without 'the qualities of being hot or cold, dry or moist, light or heavy, and of having any taste, smell, sound, colour, light, or other such quality'; but, in contrast to the subtleties of the philosophers, he will consider it 'as a real, perfectly solid body which uniformly fills the entire length, breadth and depth of this huge space' (p. 91). Anticipating the theses of the *Principles*, the concepts of space and extension serve as a strategic premise for the definition of matter:

> The whole difficulty [the philosophers] face with their matter arises simply from their wanting to distinguish it from its own quantity and from its external extension—that is, from the property it has of occupying space (p. 92) [. . .] [in such a way that] each of its parts always occupies a part of that

space which it fits so exactly that it could neither fill a larger one nor squeeze into a smaller; nor could it, while remaining there, allow another body to find a place there (p. 91).

This property, the *estenduë*, is not an accident of matter, but 'its true form and essence' (p. 92). Aristotle's *hulē*, the unformed potentiality to assume all forms, and Plato's *khōra*, the medium between the intelligible and the sensible—which is so difficult to conceive that we

seem nearly to perceive it in dreams with a sort of bastard reasoning—are reduced, with a gesture that is as drastic as it is arbitrary, to the property of occupying a space. This is why 'there is nothing simpler or easier to know' (p. 91) than matter; this is why being or having a body straightforwardly means: being extended.

'God of Abraham, God of Isaac, God of Jacob, not of the philosophers and the learned,' we read in the 'Memorial' that Pascal always carried with him. According to Pascal, Descartes 'would fain have managed to dispense with God throughout his philosophy; but he could not help letting Him give a fillip to get the world going. That done, he has no further use for Him' (p. 161). The God of the philosophers is not the God of the Christians, who is 'not simply the author of geometric truths and the order of the elements', but a God

> of love and consolation, a God who fills the soul and heart of those whom he hath purchased, a God who makes them deeply conscious of their misery and of His infinite mercy; who makes His home in their heart, filling it with humility, joy, confidence and love; who renders them incapable of any other object than Himself (pp. 6–9).

In the same sense, Heidegger can write that 'Man can neither pray nor offer sacrifice to this god. Before the *causa sui*, man can neither fall to his knees in awe nor can he play music and dance before this god' (Heidegger, p. 72). What Pascal and Heidegger say about the god of the philosophers can also be said of the body of the philosophers, which is not a living body but a 'stretch' that occupies a certain geometric space and is in no way distinguished from a 'statue or machine made of earth, which God forms with the explicit intention of making it as much as possible like us' (Descartes, p. 99).

6. The device that allows the formation of a new image of the body is, therefore, extension—that is, a conception of space and matter that, over the course of centuries, has become so familiar that we have lost sight of its novelty. There is no better way to measure this novelty than to compare it to the Platonic doctrine of the *khōra*, which, precisely during those same years, was undergoing a significant reconsideration in the thought of More and Newton. Newton clearly saw that a critique of the Cartesian doctrine of space presupposed a refutation of his doctrine of extension. Descartes, he writes, 'seems to have demonstrated that body does not differ at all from extension, abstracting hardness, colour, weight, cold, heat, and the remaining qualities which body can lack, so that at least there remains only its extension in length, width and depth, which therefore alone pertain to its essence' (Newton, p. 21). It is precisely this reduction of the body to extension that Newton intends to refute, aware that this meant shaking the very 'principal foundation of Cartesian philosophy' (p. 21). While Descartes had identified substance with extension, Newton's peremptory thesis is that extension is neither a substance nor an accident, but 'has its own manner of existing' (*proprium existendi modum*), which is none other than an 'emanative

effect of God' and 'an affection of every kind of being' (p. 21). The expression *effectus emanativus* derives from Henry More, who had been his teacher at Oxford and who called emanative effect an affection produced by something 'merely by [its] Being, [with] no other activity of causality interposed' (More, *Immortality*, p. 37). This means that a body does not occupy a space, but space emanates, so to speak, from the body, as if the body necessarily exists by spreading itself out. Or as in that extraordinary conception of extension in Robert Grosseteste's treatise on light, in which light diffuses and extends matter, dragging it along with itself.

Against Hobbes, and taking up his precise terms in order to overthrow them, Newton states that space 'is not an imaginary being, but is real, indeed divine', not 'the phantasm of an existent thing as existent' (*phantasma rei existentis quatenus existentis*), but rather 'an affection of a being just as being' (Newton, p. 25). This coincides with the ubiquity of God; indeed, it is the 'emanative effect of the first existing being, for if any being whatsoever is posited, space is posited' (p. 25). This does not mean that space is the body of God or that 'God [is] like a body, extended and made of divisible parts' (p. 26). The question about space is rather about the mode of its presence in the world, which is the very presence of God in the world: not something that God ever needed to create but, so to speak, his inseparable 'sensorium', through which he feels and knows that world, and through which we too feel and know bodies. We can perceive bodies because they are perceived at every moment by God, ranging over his sensorium.

Space is not a material extension; exactly the opposite: it is the knowability of bodies, their opening themselves and revealing themselves to view, something that is essentially immaterial and incorporeal. And it is in this sense that More recalls that the Kabbalists called God 'place' ('*ipsum divinum Numen apud Cabbalistas appellari Makom, id est locum*') (More, *Enchiridion Metaphysicum*, p. 70).

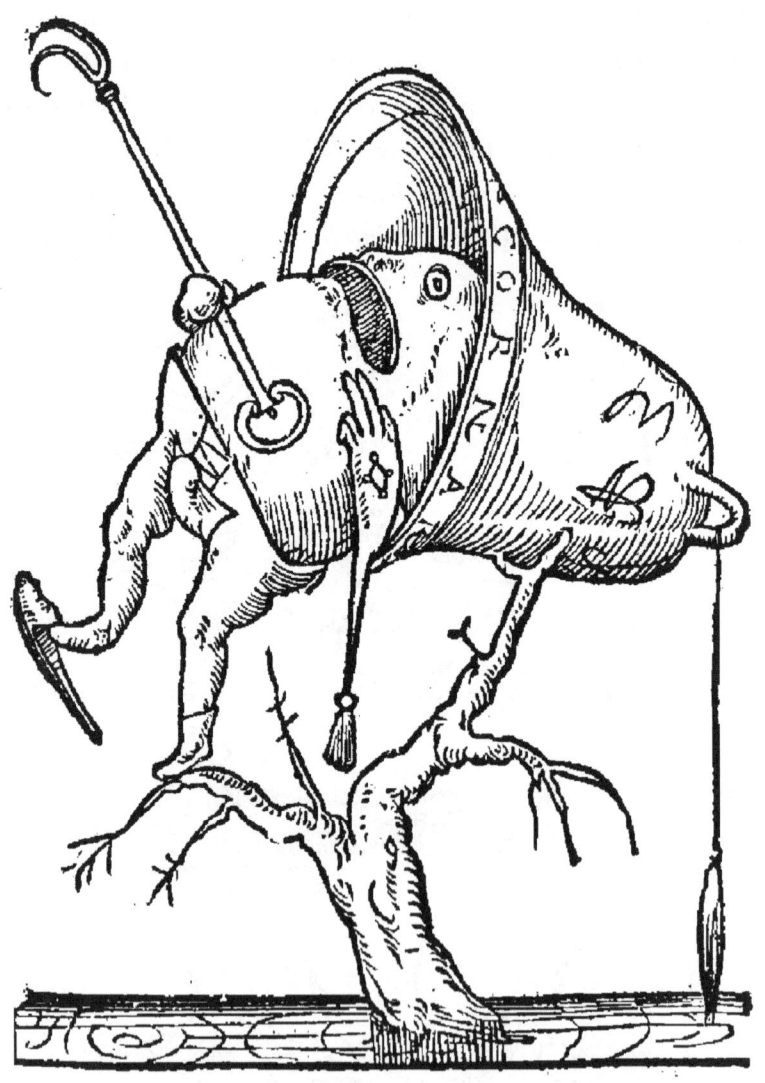

By reforming the concept of space, Descartes did not merely touch upon a problem of physics; rather, he changed the very status of truth. *Spatium*, from *pateo* (I am open) is the 'patentness', the knowability and openness of beings—in a word: their truth. Being knowable and open now comes to be understood as *estenduë*, extension, and this gets identified with matter. The knowable is always already known, spread out and measured. The body is not a *monstrum*, a marvel that shows itself and lets itself be seen, but a certain measurable portion of occupied space.

7. If God and the world are, so to speak, coextensive, and the space in which things and bodies appear to lie is both the very presence of God and the sensorium in which he perceives them, then it is possible that Rabelais and Folengo had something like this in mind when they described the exuberant body of their heroes and their language. The bodies of the giants, in keeping with their origins in an immoderate swelling, are not defined portions of geometric space, but an uninterrupted spreading out that drags itself along, moves and exposes itself in all directions. Just as incessantly do the outside and inside mix and blur within them without hesitation or restraint. There is not a single bollock, but hundreds of bollocks, following one another in a sort of doxological litany (*couillon moisy, couillon rouy, couillons chaumeny, couillon poitry d'eau froide, coiullon pendillant, couillon transy, couillon avallé, couillon guavache* . . .); there

is not one organ or member of Quarêmeprenant, but hundreds of anatomical exhibits in an immense inorganography:

> nails, like a gimlet; heels, like a mace; knees, like a stool; a navel, like a hurdy-gurdy; an arsehole, like a crystalline looking-glass; the cheeks of his arse, like a harrow; armpits, like a chessboard; elbows, like rat-traps; a nose, like cothurns fastened with escutcheons; temples, like a watering-can; eyes, like a case for combs; skin, like a sieving-cloth . . . . if he gobbed, it was basketfuls of wild artichokes; if he wiped off his snot, it was salted eels; if he belched, it was oysters-in-their-shells; if he farted, it was brown cowhide gaiters; if he tickled himself, it was fresh precepts . . . . (Rabelais, pp. 755–58)

(This blend of organic and inorganic will be recalled by the inventor of the extraordinary engravings of the *Songes drolatiques de Pantagruel*—who may have been Rabelais himself—in which implements of all kinds are hybridized with human bodies).

Numbers and quantities are always exaggerated: with a single piss, Gargantua drowns 260,418 men, not including women and children. To nurse him as a newborn, it took the milk of 17,913 cows. As for the baby Pantagruel, we know that at every meal he sucked the milk of 4,600 cows. Exaggerated and multiplied to such a degree, numbers and measurements lose their value and no longer count or measure anything. And if there is no way to distinguish the immense landscape in Pantagruel's mouth from the world, it is because the world does not exist—only and always worlds within worlds that fall into one another's abyss in an endless blazon, which is the very sensibility of God as a living and thinking being.

Chapter Three

Stultitia loquitur

1.

> *Regula Donati, prunis, salcicia coxit;*
> *ivit et in centum scartozzos Norma Perotti.*
> *Quid Catholiconis malnetta vocabula dicam,*
> *quae quot habent letras tot habent menchionica verba,*
> *et quot habent cartas tot culos illa netarent?*
>
> He cooked sausages on coals of Donatus's *Rule*;
> And Perotti's *Standard* went into a hundred pieces of scrap
>   paper.
> What shall I say of the wicked terms of the *Catholicon*,
> which have as many foolish words as they have letters,
> and would wipe as many butts as they have pages?
> (Folengo, *Chaos*, p. 84; translation modified)

Among the books that the young Baldo puts to not very edifying use here, the *Regula Donati* is certainly the *Ars grammatica* of Aelius Donatus (fourth century), the indispensable model, along with Priscian's *Institutiones grammaticae*, for every grammatical study of Latin. But who is Perotti, and what are the *malnetta vocabula Catholiconis*, so useful for excremental hygiene? The *Catholicon* is the Latin dictionary composed by the Genoese Giovanni Balbi, completed in 1286, which, up to its first printed edition in 1460, was for nearly two centuries the principal lexical resource for Latin, consulted by both Petrarch and the first Italian humanists. As for the *Norma Perotti*, the phrase might refer to the *Rudimenta grammaticae* (1468) of Niccolò Perotti, archbishop of Siponto, but more probably to the *Cornu copiae seu lingua latinae commentarii* which the same author published in Venice in 1489. Along with Valla's *Elegantiae*, it had a great fortune in all the countries of Europe. Commenting on the poets—above all Martial—Perotti acrobatically ranges far and wide across the Latin lexicon, linking together terms whose affinity is often the fruit of the author's metaphoric ingenuity. Thus, the adjective *barbarus* calls back to *blesus* and *balbus* ('stammering', *balbuziente*), but also *barbarismus*, *metaplasmus*, and *solecismus* (incorrect usages of language), then to *imparilitas* and *scribligo*, which have to do with the improper use of words. From here we jump to *scriblita*, a kind of tart, to beards (*barbae*), to Solon the sage and various kinds of fish and goats, all the way up to a type of lyre (*barbitos*) (Moss, p. 20).

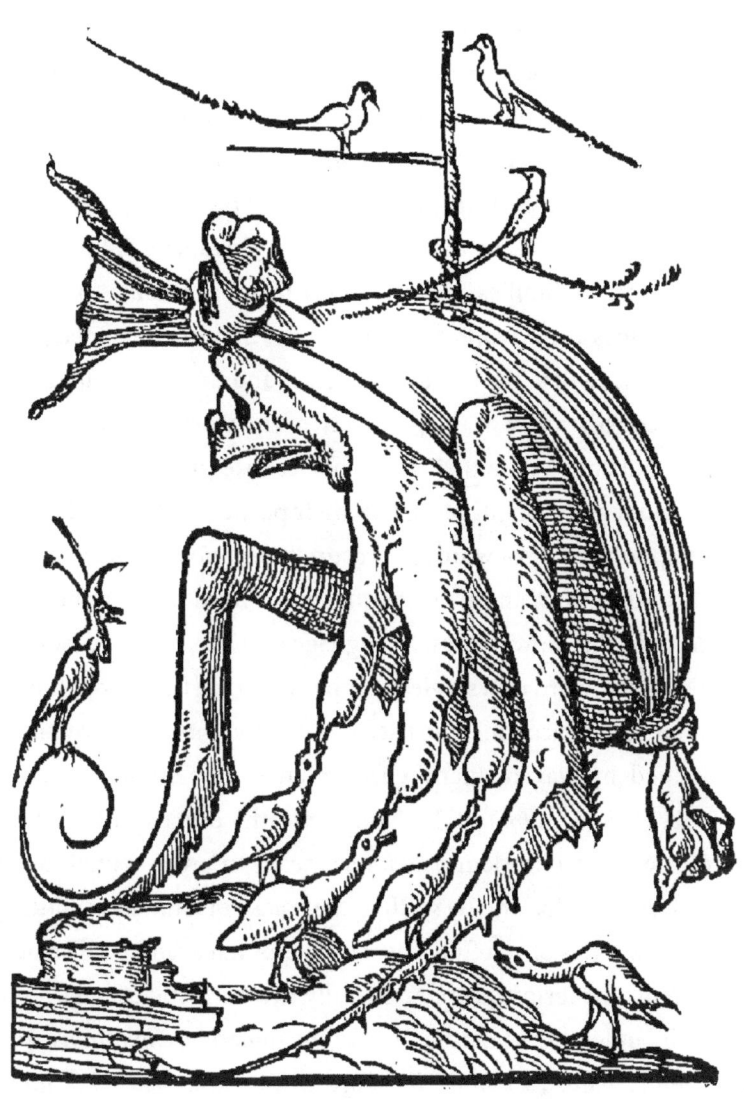

Perotti, who certainly did not imagine he would end up in Folengo's hundred 'pieces of scrap paper', does not justify his fantastic lexical excursions. But about four decades later, a friend of Rabelais, Étienne Dolet, in the two volumes of his *Commentarii linguae latinae* (1536 and 1538), is perfectly aware that he is proposing a new lexicographic paradigm. His dictionary is not alphabetical, but rather gathers words in families or sematic territories according to a principle he defines as *translatio*, but which is much more than metaphor. He is convinced that 'the beauty (*venustas*) and the use of a language does not consist solely in the propriety of the words (*in vocum proprietate*), but above all in their metaphorical use (*in translatis... dictionis*)' and that 'all languages obtain their particular dignity through the metaphorical use of words (*ex vocum translatione*)' (Moss, p. 28). That is to say, the meaning of a word is not a fixed point; rather, it is a *continuum* that flows through language and can never be isolated within a single word or a single morpheme. 'Once the proper meaning, the metaphorical one, the use, and variety of the constructions, are defined by way of many Ciceronian examples,' he writes, 'I immediately add (*subjungo*, lit. 'yoke beneath') other words that are akin in meaning'. If the lemma *odorari* means to 'grasp something by its smell, as dogs do, who by sniffing the tracks of animals eventually find them', a series of carefully chosen Ciceronian examples displaces and extends the term (*translatio* literally means 'displacement') into a virtually indefinite semantic *continuum*: *quaerere, explorare, expiscari, contari, scitari, sciscitari, indagare, investigare, olfacere, scrutari, elicere* . . . Dolet's *Commentarii* finally end with a series of lexical clusters that recall the accumulation of synonyms Spitzer precisely documented in Rabelais.

2. We should thus pause a moment on the friendship that links Rabelais to this humanist, poet and editor (in 1542 he published *La plaisante, Joyeuse histoyre du grand Geant Gargantua*, which was copied from the Paris edition of 1537), who would end up burned at the stake for heresy in Paris at only thirty-seven years of age.

Rabelais probably met him in Lyon in 1534, when Dolet was trying to publish the first volume of his *Commentarii* and Rabelais his *Gargantua*. It is more than likely, as has been suggested, that Dolet spoke with his friend about his revolutionary way of conceptualizing a dictionary and that Rabelais was not indifferent to the metaphorical nets that his friend was casting over the Latin lexicon. In any case, it is something similar to what Rabelais will do with French, multiplying metaphorical lists and connections to an unbelievable degree.

Beyond the stylistic and literary ends that Spitzer focuses on, what is at stake in this unique linguistic practice that never ceases to amuse and astonish readers? Nothing less that a new conception of language. Pushing his friend's paradigm of *Cornu copia* to the extreme, Rabelais transforms the entire Aristotelian idea of language as 'signifying voice'. He shows, through the accumulation of related words, that there does not exist *a* meaning, but an infinitely varying series of meanings in motion, similar to a wave that flows through the ocean of language. Not only are the identity and fixedness of the semantic brought into question, but also those of the semiotic, dissolved in a tangle of assonances that ceaselessly blend into one another. If the dictionary, by fixing the lexicon, dammed up and contained the linguistic flux by compartmentalizing it in an ordered list of lemmas each with its own record, Rabelais, putting Dolet's example to good use, blows up the identity of all words, which cease to be 'terms'—that is, something circumscribed by a border—and dissolve into a semantic–semiotic *continuum* in which both signifier and signified blur and fade. Language as a whole becomes this *translatio*, this tireless and, quite literally, 'boundless' movement of meanings and sounds, endlessly articulated (or rather, disarticulated) by the mouths of giants and buffoons.

Once again, that is not a poetic choice but a conception of language that has its theoretical basis in the doctrine of the philosophers of the fourteenth century, like Gregory of Rimini, who held that what is at issue in language is not the proposition (the *enuntiatum*, formed by a subject, a copula and a predicate) or an object existing outside of the mind corresponding to the word designating it, but something he calls *complexe significabile* or *enuntiabile*, the 'signifiable in a complex way' or signifiable complex, whose particular mode of being he tries to define beyond being and non-being, beyond the mind and extramental reality. In a passage of the *Categories* (12b5–16), Aristotle had written that while affirmations and negations (for example, 'he is sitting' or 'he is not sitting') are statements (*logoi*), the thing (*pragma*) at issue in these (which Aristotle expresses with the infinitive: 'to be sitting' or 'not to be sitting') is not a statement. Commenting on this passage, Gregory deduces from it that what are true or false are not the propositions, much less the real things, but that 'stateable', or signifiable plexus, which he expresses with an infinitive proposition: not 'the man is white' but 'the man to be white' (or 'the man not to be white').

What's decisive here is the way Gregory conceives of the substance of this *tertium*, which, insofar as it coincides with neither the proposition nor the signified object, risks appearing as a nothing. The 'thing' at issue in the true proposition 'the man is white' is neither, Gregory suggests, the thing 'man' nor the thing 'white', nor is it their logical conjunction through the copula, but rather a *res sui generis*: the 'man-to be-white', which lies neither in the mind nor in reality, but somehow beyond existence and non-existence. Thus, even in the case of the metaphysical thesis 'God is' (*Deus est*) the stateable (or *complexe significabile*) that corresponds to it—'God-to be' (*Deum esse*)—'is not something other, that is, another entity with respect to God (*alia entitas guam Deus*), and yet, it is not God nor, in general, any entity' (Gregory of Rimini, *Commentary on the Sentences*, BOOK 1, DIST. 1, QUEST. 1, ART. 1). The being of language—as Meinong would understand many centuries later—is beyond being and non-being.

It is possible that Rabelais had a 'complex' of this sort in mind when in the ramblings of his characters he puts into question the identity of words. The body of language is made up of an infinity of words serially thrown together, which do not separate themselves as organs of a body to form a single organism, but rather, as happens in the immense body of the giants, give up their singular consistency in order to multiply and obliterate themselves in a continuous and virtually limitless complex.

3. By one of those coincidences in which an unknown nemesis is at work, a somewhat similar fate was reserved for Dolet's very name. In a copy of his work held in the Biblioteca Angelica in Rome (the former library of the Augustinians), every time the name Doletus appears it is precisely covered by a little strip of paper on which is written the word *Deletus* (that is, 'erased', as a consequence of the infamy that befell heretics burned at the stake). The play on words would not have displeased Rabelais—and perhaps not his friend either—as the first examples in a series of indefinitely extendable terms: *dolens, dolentia, dolium* (cask), *olentia, olfacere*, all the way up to *oletum* (excrement).

The threat of heresy loomed over Rabelais as well. It is not by chance that in his *De scandalis*, Calvin cites *Rabelaesus* among those who 'have had to do with the faith (*gustato Evangelio*)' but who, 'struck by blindness', have sacrilegiously profaned the 'sacred pledge of eternal life' 'for the recklessness of play and laughter (*ludendi aut ridendi audacia*)', and elsewhere he calls him, along with Dolet, a 'dog' and a 'pig'. And it was to escape the Inquisition that, in 1547, after the first two books had been condemned by the Sorbonne, Rabelais had to move to Italy, relying on the protection of Jean du Bellay.

The fact is that conceptions of language are neither theologically, nor philosophically, nor politically neutral. In a language that has put into question the identity of the name and the concept, even the consistency of theological concepts becomes precarious. How can we hold fast the identity of divine persons once names begin slipping into one another? And how can we attribute a certain action to a certain subject once both language and the world have become a continuous and unstoppable flux?

We find further proof of the risks entailed in a certain use of language in the influence Rabelais's language exercised on another philosopher burned at the stake for heresy, Giordano Bruno. Scholars have retraced more than one analogy between passages from *The Ash Wednesday Supper*, *The Candlemaker* and *The Expulsion of the Triumphant Beast* and corresponding episodes in *Gargantua*, which Bruno had probably read during his first trip to France, between 1579 and 1581, in Paris, Toulouse, and more likely in Lyon, where Rabelais had worked as a doctor and had published some of his work. But the place of Rabelais's true influence on Bruno is language. Reading the first dialogue in one of the Nolan's most philosophically dense works, *Cause, Principle and Unity*, it is difficult to imagine a prose more baldly Rabelaisian than the ramblings of Filoteo, the character with whom Bruno seems to identify:

> You, shield-bearers of Pallas, standard-bearers of Minerva, Mercury's stewards; you, Jupiter's custodians, Apollo's milk brothers, Epimetheus' co-thieves, Bacchus' bottlers, Euhancriers' horse-grooms; you, who scourge the Edonides, spur on the Thyiades, excite the Maenads, seduce the Bassarids;

you, the riders of the Mimallonides, copulators of the Egerian nymph, moderators of enthusiasm, demagogues of wandering peoples, decipherers of the Demogorgon, Dioscures of fluctuating disciplines, treasurers of the Pantamorpheus and bullock-emissaries of the highpriest Aron: to you we recommend our prose, submit our Muses, our premises, subsumptions, digressions, parentheses, applications, clauses, periods, constructions, adjectives and epithets. O you, sugarwater vendors, who ravish our spirits with your sweet little refinements, binding fast our hearts, fascinating our minds, and delivering our prostituted souls to the lupanar; you, who submit our barbarisms to your wise judgement, stick our solecisms with your arrows, staunch our malodorous chasms, castrate our Silenes, clap our Noahs into breeches, emasculate our macrological discourses, patch up our ellipses, curb our tautologies, temper our acyrologies, excuse our escrologies, pardon our perissologies, forgive our cacophonies. (Bruno, pp. 31–32)

And no less Pantagruelian is the delirious list that follows a few pages later:

[T]he philosopher [Aristotle], wishing to elucidate what primary matter is, compares it to the female sex—that sex, I mean, which is intractable, frail, capricious, cowardly, feeble, vile, ignoble, base, despicable, slovenly, unworthy, deceitful, harmful, abusive, cold, misshapen, barren, vain, confused, senseless, treacherous, lazy, fetid, foul, ungrateful, truncated, mutilated, imperfect, unfinished, deficient, insolent, amputated, diminished, stale, vermin, tares, plague, sickness, death. (p. 72)

Only in a language that had so thoroughly questioned every semantic identity and every distinction was it possible to conceive of the infinite vicissitudes of the universe, as Bruno describes them in the dialogue.

4. 'I called you father, but I could also say mother, if your indulgence will permit me . . . everything that I am and that I am worth, I received from you alone': so writes Rabelais to Erasmus on 30 November 1532, just two months after the publication in Lyon of the *Horribles et espouvantables faicts et prouesses du tresrenommé Pantagruel Roi des Dipsodes* (The horrible and terrifying deeds and words of the very renowned Pantagruel, King of the Dipsodes). From that point on, Sorbonigenes and Linceiforms have with stubborn pedantry compiled meticulous lists of phrases that Rabelais is said to have paraphrased or copied from Erasmus, beginning with the famous passage about the *Sileni* that opens the prologue to *Gargantua*, as if the influence of one writer on another could be measured by counting words. The fact is—as Rabelais is not afraid to confess, declaring himself the 'most ungrateful of all men who ever existed and will exist in the future' if he were not to admit his debt to

the *pater amatissimus*—he has done nothing in his books but rewrite the *Praise of Folly*. We cannot understand Rableais if we do not first understand that at the head of each of his books, too, we could write the inscription: *Stultitia loquitur*. Nothing is more instructive in this regard than reading the prologue to *Gargantua* alongside the letter to Thomas More that opens the *Praise of Folly*. The warning to the 'most shining of drinkers [and] most be-carbuncled of syphilitics' not to allow themselves to be fooled by burlesque titles 'such as *Gargantua, Pantagruel, on the Merits of Codpieces, On Pease-pudding and Bacon, with a Latin Commentary*' into 'too readily conclud[ing] that nothing is treated inside save jests, idiocies and amusing fictions' (Rabelais, p. 206) corresponds perfectly to the warning in the letter to More against 'contentious fellows' who will 'cavil . . . that these trifles are more frivolous than befits a theologian' (Erasmus, p. 2). The evocation of the 'substantificial marrow' that the reader, like the dog, *la beste du monde plus philosophique*, must know how to extract from the marrow-bone in order to realize that what it 'contains is of a very different value from that which its box ever promised' (Rabelais, p. 207) recalls Erasmus's assertion that 'fooleries may be so handled that a reader who is not altogether a fathead may garner more of profit from them than from the bristling and pompous arguments of some whom we know' (Erasmus, p. 3). Certainly, at issue is a strong poetic claim for the humorous form, placed in a genealogy which Rabelais traces back to Homer and Ovid, but which Erasmus for his part declines in a meticulous list that ends with a character who seems to come straight out of a Pantagruelian book:

> Let any, however, who are offended by the lightness and foolery of my argument remember, I beg, that mine is not the first example, but that the same thing was often practised by great authors. Homer, all those ages ago, made sport with a battle of frogs and mice; Virgil, with a gnat, and a salad; Ovid, with a nut. Polycrates eulogized Busiris; and Isocrates, though a castigator of Polycrates, did the same; Glaucon argued in praise of injustice; Favorinus, of Theristes and of the quartan fever; Synesius, of baldness; Lucian, of the fly and of the parasite. Seneca sported with an Apotheosis of the Emperor Claudius; Plutarch, in a dialogue between Gryllus and Ulysses; Lucian and Apuleius, with an ass; and someone whom I do not know, with the last will and testament of Grunius Corocotta, a hog. (Erasmus, p. 2)

This is not simply a literary legitimization: for both it is essential to situate themselves, by giving a voice to folly, at a threshold of indifference between truth and invention, between theological dogma and mythical tale, between parrhesia and lie—a sort of free zone in which it is possible to speak truthfully as if one were mad and to ramble on as if one were reasoning. This is the brilliant feat of Erasmus's *Praise of Folly*, in which the reader never knows until the end whether they are dealing with a sincere encomium or a condemnation without any possible appeal. In reality, it is obviously neither one nor the other so much as the isolation of the linguistic statement removed from the true/false alternative, which defines the *logos apophantikos* that Western logic received in inheritance, along with outstanding debts, from Aristotle. *Stultitia loquitur*: but once it is folly that is speaking, we must abide by the character of the personage—or by its mask: *quam cum loquentem fecerimus, decoro personae serviendum fui* ('since I have feigned her speaking, it was of course necessary to preserve decorum in her character') (Erasmus, p. 4), as Erasmus writes with a gesture that is analogous but symmetrically opposite to Descartes's *larvatus prodeo* ('I go forth masked'). Where the latter believed he had found a place in which truth became certain, Erasmus and Rabelais shift their speech to a site in which every *certitudo* is excluded, in which the truth is always at risk between laughter and prophesy, between *l'aise du corps* and *mystères horrifiques*. Like the surname of Thomas More, which comes as close to the word *folly* (*tam ad moriae vocabulum accredit*) as he himself is far from it.

Only if the reader is able to situate themselves in this special place of enunciation, where the alternative between false or true is at least provisionally suspended, is it possible to correctly read both the testament of Grunius Corocotta and the chronicles of Pantagruel. The truth in question here does not concern the content of the statement, but the statement itself: what is true is not the *dictum* but the act of saying [*dire*] itself. Thus the truth of both the discourse of folly and the words of Pantagruel or Panurge does not match up to a correspondence with facts—which, after all, is impossible—but rather an experiment in which what is always in play is not the verification or non-verification of something, but the very place in which truth will be able to exist. This place is language—more precisely: its body. The Pantagruelian experiment succeeds if language takes on a body, beyond or before its signifying something, its saying something about something. Language that is no longer a sign, but body and voice, victoriously resists its construction in a grammatical system—just as it resists the presupposition of a thinking subject that entrusts its reality to a disembodied *cogito*. Pantragruel is not the locutor presupposed to his verbocinations. Pantagruel's body is the body of his language. And only in this sense *Pantagruel loquitur*.

5. Hence the impertinence of the debates that split interpreters into those, like Bakhtin, who see Rabelais as a flagrant supporter of the low, who avidly calls up all its gastric and excremental aspects, and those who instead read his chronicles as a hidden itinerary towards the high and the sublime. No less incongruous is the division between the champions of a Rabelais soaked in medieval theology (an exemplary case being the acute monograph by Gilson) and the proponents of a rationalist and Renaissance Pantagruel. Rabelais's first invention is a world in which these oppositions no longer make sense: bollocks are very high and propitious, while quintessence is meagre and mired (or better: Alcofribas is precisely the one who knows how to distil

bollocks from quintessence, that is, render their dispute moot). Homer is a contemporary while the *Sorbillans* and *Sorbonagres* he has to deal with are resolutely medieval.

This conscious neutralization of the load-bearing dichotomies of our culture assails every sphere and milieu, from theology to morals, from politics to rhetoric, including that science of which Rabelais, as a doctor and anatomist, was the representative *in partibus literatorum*. It is enough for him to over-detail anatomical descriptions to drain them of credibility:

> Whereupon he sliced through his head at one blow, cutting his cranium above the petrous bone, removing both the bones of the sinciput as well as the sagittal suture, together with the greater part of the coronal bone; by so doing he sliced through both meninges and opened up deeply the two posterior ventricle-cavities of the brain: and so his cranium remained hanging down over his shoulders at the back from the membranes of the pericranium in the form of a doctoral bonnet, black above, red within. (Rabelais, p. 340)

The supreme sphere of this confusion of terms is, obviously, language. The opposition between lexicon and syntax, semiotic and semantic, hypotaxis and parataxis plunges into an abyss in which names, spreading and multiplying in an infinite series, give up all claims to the syntactical articulation of discourse. Rabelais, like Folengo in his way, has formed a new body for language which, shedding its old grammatical shell, can now, like a butterfly joyously leaving the cocoon, explore new—or rather, prehistoric—territories of thought.

Chapter Four

Self-Parody

1. The buffoon and the rogue are consanguineous in some way. This common bloodline is something well known to the picaro, who inherits their legacy and preserves a form of innocence to the end. Margutte's long self-introduction compiles its canon and pandects as proof that he is 'a true descendant of [his] folks' and that one should 'plant no vineyard on these rocks [his land]'. Born as he was of a Greek nun and 'holy pope from Bursia' in Turkey, after a quarrel in a mosque he slew his father and 'took a stroll around the whole wide world':

> and my companion friends have been but these—
> all of my sins from Turkey and from Greece—
> or, better yet, as many as are in hell.
> My mortal sins are seventy and seven,
> Which—winter, summer—never leave my sight.

> My venial ones? You count them if you can!
> If even this our world should endless be,
> no one, I swear, commits as many sins
> as I did in this life of mine commit:
> I know my trade just like the alphabet. (Pulci, p. 365)

The sins, though, are not all that mortal, since they consist essentially—if he has a bit of money—of gambling with dice 'or draw[ing] flame or cross, or head or cat' as well as a shameless gluttony that anticipates the binges of Pantagurel.

> Gluttony is the second of my arts.
> Here your discernment you must use: indeed,
> you must the page of every secret know,
> concerning pheasants, partridges, and capons,
> and all the delicacies in each detail,
> in search of the most succulent delight:
> none of my words would ever fail in this—
> to keep your palate wet and full of bliss. (Pulci, p. 366)

At first glance, Baldo's misdeeds seem far graver. He is the leader of a gang that includes the two great scoundrels Cingar and Fracasso and a half-man, half-dog monster named Falchetto. But here, too, the rogue, like the picaro, proves ultimately innocent, as his villainies soon turn into a kind of fairytale journey of initiation, which ends in a descent to an inferno shaped like a pumpkin, *seccam busamque dedentrum* (dry and empty inside), where the former rogue might even end up settling with his author, Merlin Cocaio. What all these characters have in common is that it is decidedly impossible for them to live a life 'of their own'; they can only, in a formula with which Americo Castro defines the existence of the picaro, unlive it, *vivir desviviendose*, stubbornly denying their own essence and their own identity at every moment. This means that in them collapses the fundamental literary convention that a novel must tell how characters live their lives. Neither Margutte nor Baldo nor Pantagruel are characters in this sense. They live, brazenly and at full tilt, without having a life of their own.

2. There are various ways to unlive one's life. One is that of the picaro, but another, no less wild-eyed and fatal, is that of the *hidalgo*, Don Quixote. By now it seems certain that Cervantes had read Folengo, and it is not difficult to imagine the young *estudiante*, having fled to Italy in 1569 to escape the accusation *de haber herido en duelo a un maestro de obras llamado Antonio de Sigura*, leafing with surprise and delight through the macaronic poems, which were at that time in wide circulation. A recent study, to which we will return, has compared the concluding episode of *Baldo*, the descent into the hellish pumpkin, with chapters 22–23 of the second part of the *Quixote*, which describes an analogous hellish adventure of the knight errant in the cave of Montesinos. It is curious, however, that two other parallels—quite striking ones—have not been previously noted. In the third book of *Baldo* the young *cativellus*, who has begun to attend

school *non spontaneus* (only when he felt like it), as soon as he begins to 'poke his nose into' the books about Orlando (*Orlandi nasare volumina coepit*), throws away the grammar books and 'scrap paper' of the pedants and dives into his reading of books about chivalry.

> *Orlandi tantum gradant et gesta Rinaldi*
> *... Legerat Ancroiam, Tribisondam, facta Danesi,*
> *Antonnaeque Bovum, Antiforra, realia Franzae*
> *innamoramentum Carlonis et Asperamontem*
> *Spagnam, Altobellum, Morgantis bella gigantis*
> *Meschinique provas et qui Cavalerius Orsae*
> *dicitur et nulla cecinit qui laude leandram.*
> *Vidut ut Angelicam sapiens Orlandus amavit*
> *utque caminavit nudo cum corpore mattus ...*

Only the exploits of Orlando and Rinaldo please him ...
He has read the *Ancroia*, the *Trebisonda*, *Ogier the Dane*,
Bovo d'Antona, *Antiforra*, the *Reali di Francia*,
Il libro dell'innamoramento di Rè Carlo, *Aspramonte*,
Spagna, *Altobello*, the battles of the giant Morgante,
   the deeds of Guerrin Meschino, the one called Cavaliere
      dell'Orsa,
and the inglorious poetry of *Leandra*.
He sees how wise Orlando loved Angelica
and how he travelled naked and crazed ...
(Folengo, *Baldo*, VOL. 1, pp. 74–75)

In this list, which has rightly been defined as a 'small anti-canon of Chivalric literature' (Perrotta, p. 19), we find *Orlando*, the *Trebisonda*, the *Ancroia*, *Bovo d'Antona*, the *Reali di Francia*, *Guerrin Meschino*, all the books that the good *hidalgo* in 'his times of leisure—which meant most of the year' (Cervantes, p. 20)—had surely learnt by heart up to the point of losing his mind. And it is at the very least notable that Baldo lingers on the episode of Orlando's madness, where he *caminavit nudus cum corpore mattus*, just as in chapters 25 and 26 the first part, Don Quixote strips himself naked and commits mad acts in imitation of Orlando, whose jealousy of Angelica has made him crazy. And like Don Quixote, Baldo, too, *in his factis nimium stigatur ad arma*, 'is fiercely spurred by such feats to take up arms', even if the smallness of his body makes him sad (*sed tantum quod sit piccolettus corpore tristat*). And just as the adventurous *hidalgo* will dust off his rusty armour and morion missing its visor, so too Baldo *armiculam portat gallone taccatam / qui facit ad signum molesinos stare bravazzos* ('carries a little sword at his side that frightens bullies and puts them in their place') (Folengo, *Baldo*, VOL. 1, pp. 74-75).

No less surprising is another parallel, this time of a, so to speak, metaliterary nature. Everyone remembers how in the prologue to the second book of the *Quixote* Cervantes addresses the reader, evoking 'the author of the second *Don Quixote* . . . the one sired in Tordesillas, they say, and born in Tarragona'.

You would like me to call him an ass, a fool, an insolent dolt, but the thought has not even entered my mind: let his sin be his punishment, let him eat it with his bread, and let that be an end to it. (Cervantes, p. 455)

At issue here is the *Segundo tomo del ingenioso hidalgo Don Quijote de la Mancha* 'composed not by Cide Hamete Benengeli . . . but by an Aragonese who is, he says, a native of Tordesillas' (Cervantes, p. 916). The impostor, whom Cervantes does not even name, is Alonso Fernandez Avellaneda, who published his apocryphal text in 1614. In truth, though, through the whole second volume of the *Quixote*, Don Quixote and Sancho maintain a subtle metaliterary dialogue with this unnamed author, whose book is finally thrown by the devils 'into the pit of hell', for just as they are aware of their adventures narrated in the first volume, they are careful to disavow the tales invented by the impostor.

As it happens, the preface to the Toscolanese edition of the *Baldo* opens with an *epistolium colericum* in which the *magister* Acquario Lodola apostrophizes the 'disemboweled' Scardaffo Zaratono, who is guilty of having stolen, corrupted and falsified Merlin Cocaio's macaronic poem.

> *Tu tamen fraudolenter me inadvertente poema praeclarissimi Merlini Cocaii macaronicum robasti, corrupisti, falsificati et multa non sua interposuisti et plures libros surripuisti, quos tibi tribuere volebas, manigolde, furcifer malignissime.*

> Yet you fraudulently, while I was not paying attention, stole the macaronic poem of the most illustrious Merlin Cocaio; you corrupted it, falsified it, and interpolated many things that were not his, and you pilfered many books which you

wanted to attribute to yourself, you rogue, you most wicked scoundrel. (Folengo, *Le Maccheronee*, p. 275).

It would be a work welcome by God, the writer of the preface adds, *te scortegare, homo pessime, non homo sed bestia, diabolazze* (for you to be flayed, you worst of men, nay not man but beast, you great devil), who has published such an *imboazzatum* (botched) and *castratum* (mutilated) book.

3. The study that we have cited without naming the author is 'Zucche e antri infernali: considerazioni metaletterarie tra Folengo e Cervantes' (Pumpkins and infernal caves: Metaliterary considerations between Folengo and Cervantes). The author, Federica Zoppi, rightly compares the descent into hell that concludes the *Baldo* with Don Quixote's dark sojourn in the *cueva de Montesinos*. After a long series of semi-fabulous adventures, which lead him, among other things, to cross a magic forest and to find himself sailing on a giant whale, the wind blows Baldo and his companions all the way to a cave, which is in reality 'the house of fantasy' (Folengo, *Baldo*, VOL. 2, pp. 472–73), governed by a *norma sine regula* (norm with no rules) and 'full of silent murmuring, of tacit clamor, of movement in repose' (p. 473). All over the place, phantasms, foolish ideas, dreams, thoughts with no reason, shapes of all sorts and mental images fly and flutter about. In short, it is a *gabia stultorum* (cage of fools), in which 'everyone pecks at his own brain and fishes for flies in the air'

(p. 473). In this atopic land, there live 'the people of Grammar, and the offspring of Pedagogy: the noun is here, and the verb too, the pronoun and the participle, with the rest of the gang following, namely, *huc, illuc, istuc, hinc, inde, deorsum* and *sinistrorsum* and the whole clan of *cuius*' (p. 473). Present as well are the concepts *ens, acidens, substantia, cum solegismo*, and 'this whole throng assaults the companions, just as flies assault butter or ricotta' (p. 473). Baldo and his companions try to grasp the flying words and ideas, just as babies do when in play they want to *piare manu moscas* (catch flies with their hands), but, like them, they cannot hold them in their hand and find themselves *piasse nientum*. In the end, a buffoon leads them before a sort of *machina grandis*, which turns out to be nothing other than a gourd or pumpkin—call it what you like—dry and hollow inside, with a *grande foramen* (huge hole) on one side through which Baldo and friends enter without hesitation. The pumpkin, in which the poem ends, is actually the *stanza poetraum, cantorum, astrologorum* (the abode of poets, minstrels, and astrologers) who therein sing and compose their books filled with 'fables and worthless novelties' (pp. 480–81). Their punishment (and therefore the pumpkin, too, is a sort of hell) is that instead of devils, three thousand barbers with their pliers pull as many teeth as the *bosias* (lies) they have told. It is, however, in this hellish pumpkin that the author, Merlin Cocaio, who here suddenly takes over in his own name, decides to remain, since he has no other choice than to be the poet that he is:

*Opus est hic me remanere poetam
non mihi conveniens minus est habitatio zucchae
quam qui Greghettum quendam praeponit Achillem
forzibus hectoreis*

> it is necessary for me, the poet, to remain here.
> Inhabiting the pumpkin is no less fitting for me
> than for he who champions the Greekling Achilles
> over Hector's strength (pp. 482–83).

The fact is, the poet adds, that *zucca mihi patria est* (the pumpkin is my homeland) and 'here I must lose as many teeth as the falsehoods I have put in this immense book' (p. 483).

The pumpkin—even if the careful scholar does not seem to notice it—is a clear image of language, made of nouns, verbs and all the rest of the grammatical brigade. This is why the cave in which he finds himself is defined as the 'house of fantasy' and the *conocchia* itself as a *stanza poetarum*. It is possible, then, as has been suggested by Francesco Doni, that the hellish conclusion of the poem is in some way an 'image of the ruin of the word and of life, of the insufficiency of the work and of knowledge' (Ferroni, p. 22), as if at the point where the *navis stracchissima* of macaronic poetry reaches the harbour, the laughter of Folengo could not but change into bitter irony.

4. The entrance to the cave of Montesinos is certainly hellish, cluttered as it is with thorny bushes through which Don Quixote must hack out a path with his sword, and in doing so launch a cloud of enormous crows and owls into the air. Once lowered into the depths of the cavern, the *hidalgo*, crouched on the rope coiled up like a doughnut, is initially surprised to find himself 'in the midst of the most

beautiful, pleasant, and charming meadow that nature could create or the most discerning human mind imagine' (Cervantes, p. 605), in which there appears a sumptuous palace with walls of transparent crystal and from which he sees approaching a venerable ancient who turns out to be 'the same Montesinos after whom the cave is named' (p. 606). A series of details, however, seems gradually to belie his first impression. First of all, the host's clothing is extravagant to say the least: a cloak of purple baize trailing after him on the ground, his shoulders and chest wrapped with a scholar's sash and hood of green satin, and a black Milanese cap on his head. Particularly incongruous is the rosary he holds in his hand, whose smaller beads are larger than walnuts and whose larger ones are the size of ostrich eggs. We then learn that Montesinos has removed the heart, which 'must have weighed two pounds' (p. 607), from the chest of his friend Durandarte to offer it to the lady Belerema, with whom he had been in love. The lady herself is present, but instead of being beautiful, as we expect, she has teeth that are 'few in number and crooked . . . [and] deep circles under her eyes and [a] sickly colour' (p. 609), and we learn that for many years she has not suffered 'the monthly distress common in women'—more than a living person she is a sort of ghost or yellowed corpse. Still more disappointing and even grotesque is the sudden appearance of Dulcinea along with two other peasant girls 'leaping and jumping [. . .] like nanny goats' (p. 611). What is truly unbecoming is that instead of responding to the enamoured *hidalgo*'s greeting as a noble damsel should, the peasant girl, after rudely turning her back on him, has her friend ask him to loan her half a dozen *reales*, which she urgently needs.

The descent into the infernal *cueva*, then, coincides with a merciless debasement of the chivalric universe dreamed of by Don Quixote and marks, in this sense, a turning point in the evolution of the character, who once he returns from the cave will have to begin to come to terms with reality, gradually breaking the spell of his madness.

> The *cueva*, for the literary characters who find themselves in it, and that Quixote encounters, is for all intents and purposes a hell, a deadly place in which they are imprisoned, bound to repeat the same gestures, to participate forever in a funeral procession that seems to celebrate the death of chivalry itself. Instead of poets, as in Folengo's pumpkin, here the damned are the literary characters that these poets have created. Indeed, Don Quixote descends into the *cueva*, while into the pumpkin it is the author himself, Merlin Cocaio, who claims he has found his own ideal place. (Zoppi, p. 14)

5. The pumpkinization of Merlin Cocaio and the descent of Don Quixote into the *cueva* of Montesinos thus contain an extreme reflection on language and literature—on the language of literature—which we do well to confront. Perhaps the final message of the extraordinary linguistic fury that we have tried to describe in Rabelais and Folengo entails not only a special operation on the body of language, but also

a thesis about the destiny and meaning of literature. Just as the speaking being cannot come away from its stubborn and ferocious bodily conflict with language without being defeated, so too the poet is only a poet if he measures himself against his inevitable failure. And just as Folengo and Rabelais have lastingly put into question the identity of what we usually define as 'a language', but have not thereby been able to enter into another language, so too, according to the bitter but salutary lesson of the *cueva* of Montesinos, Don Quixote can find his true name and nature only to the extent that, and in the very act in which, he strips off the false identities he has assumed in making himself a knight errant—but not a step or a movement further beyond. The healing of his chivalric madness coincides with the death of the *hidalgo*.

Language and literature are like the barber's basin, which to the eyes of the knight spellbound by his own madness appears as Mambrino's glorious helmet, just as to ordinary people it appears no more than a simple barber's basin. Literature lives only by its own ceaseless disillusionment and can hold in its hands the precious, heroic sallet only insofar as others continue to see it as a humble basin. In spite of the ceaseless oscillation from one place to another, from low to high and high to low, the truth is, at every instant, both things at once.

This means that the place of such an operation can only be parodic. Etymologically, *parody* means 'a song beside', and it is this 'beside' whose special topology we must define. Folengo's language is not Latin, but neither is it the vernacular: macaronic always stands parodically to the side of both, without ever claiming, as we believe

every language does, a grammatical identity of its own. Macaronic is not a language, and the author here finds himself in the position—the comic position par excellence—of writing without having a language. Parody is the *phantasia plus quam phantastica* (fantasy, more fantastic than ever) that the poet invokes at the beginning of his song, just as the *pancificae* (paunchy) Muses who ply him with polenta stand beside Melpomene and that *menchiona* (chump) Thalia. If fantasy is the source of language and poetic creation, then a second-order fantasy intervenes here to undo and call into question the first—but without abolishing it. True inspiration—that is, philosophy—is the revocation of inspiration, but it cannot exist without it. Philosophy is—literally and Platonically—a parody—or self-parody—of poetry; it could not exist if there were no poetry. The same goes for Rabelais's language and French; it remains beside French, in the very act of demolishing and transforming it. And if language is ultimately always the language of being, then the ontology at issue here is a parodic ontology, or a para-ontology, which is worth trying to substitute for the onto-logy that has dominated—and continues to dominate—Western culture. Being—and even more so, language—can only stand beside themselves; metaphysics—as has been suggested with a perfectly serious joke by the last, brave heir of Rabelais—is pataphysics, the science of that which is added to or stands beside metaphysics.

Note on the Illustrations

The original Italian edition (Einaudi, 2024), on which this edition is based, was designed by Viviana Gottardello in collaboration with the author.

The images reproduced on pp. *ii, viii*, 44, 64 and 84 come from the 1521 Toscolano del Garda edition of Teofilo Folengo's *Baldo*, printed by the Paganini press under the title *Opus Merlini Cocai poetae Mantuani Macaronicorum*. All other illustrations are taken from *Songes drolatiques de Pantagruel*, a suite of 120 engravings published by Richard Breton in 1565 and attributed to Rabelais.

Works Cited

BAKHTIN, Mikhail. *The Dialogic Imagination* (Michael Holquist ed., Caryl Emerson and Michael Holquist trans.). Austin: University of Texas Press, 1981.

BEMBO, Pietro. *Prose e rime* (Carlo Dionisotti ed.). Turin: UTET, 1966.

BRUNO, Giordano. *Cause, Principle and Unity* (Robert de Lucca trans.). Cambridge: Cambridge University Press, 1998.

CASSIAN, Nina. *Take my Word for It*. New York: W. W. Norton, 1998.

CERVANTES, Miguel de. *Don Quixote* (Edith Grossman trans.) New York: Ecco, 2003.

COLONNA, Francesco. *Biografia e opere* (Maria Teresa Casella and Giovanni Pozzi eds), 2 VOLS. Padua: Antnore, 1959.

DESCARTES, René. *The Philosophical Writings of Descartes*, VOL. 1 (John Cottingham et al. trans and eds). Cambridge: Cambridge University Press, 1985.

DONI, Anton Francesco. *La Zucca* (1551) in *Le novelle*, VOL. 2 (Elena Pierazzo ed.). Rome: Salerno Editrice, 2003.

ERASMUS, Desiderius. *The Praise of Folly* (Hoyt Hopewell Hudson trans.). Princeton: Princeton UP, 2015.

FERRONI, Giulio. *Dopo la fine: La condizione postuma della letteratura*. Turin: Einaudi, 1996.

FOLENA, Gianfranco. *Il linguaggio del caos: Studi sul plurilinguismo rinascimentale*. Turin: Bollati Boringhieri, 1991.

FOLENGO, Teofilo. *Baldo*, 2 VOLS (Ann E. Mullaney trans.). Cambridge, MA: Harvard University Press, 2007.

FOLENGO, Teofilo. *Chaos del Triperuno* (Ann E. Mullaney trans.). 2009. Available online: tinyurl.com/3bbaw27k.

FOLENGO, Teofilo [Merlino Cocaio]. *Le Maccheronee* (1517), VOL. 2 (Alessandro Luzio ed.). Bari: Laterza, 1911.

HEIDEGGER, Martin. *Identity and Difference* (Joan Stambaugh trans.). New York: Harper and Row, 1969.

HOBBES, Thomas. *Critique du 'De Mundo' de Thomas White* (1642) (Jean Jacquot and Harold Whitmore Jones eds). Paris: Vrin, 1973[1643].

HOBBES, Thomas. *De corpore* (Karl Schuhmann ed.). Paris: Vrin, 1999.

HOBBES, Thomas. *The Elements of Law Natural and Politic* (J. C. A. Gaskin ed.). Oxford: Oxford University Press, 1994.

HOBBES, Thomas. *Leviathan* (Richard Tuck ed.). Cambridge: Cambridge University Press, 1991.

KOYRÉ, Alexandre. *Études d'Histoire de la Pensée Philosophique*. Paris: Colin, 1961.

MELANCHTHON, Philip. 'Praise of Eloquence' in *Orations on Philosophy and Education* (Sachiko Kusukawa ed., Christine F. Salazar trans.). Cambridge: Cambridge University Press, 1999.

MIGLIORINI, Bruno. *Lingua d'oggi e di ieri*. Caltanissetta / Rome: Salvatore Sciascia, 1973.

MORE, Henry. *Enchiridion Metaphysicum, sive De rebus incorporeis*. London: Flesher, 1671.

MORE, Henry. *The Immortality of the Soul* (Alexander Jacob ed.). Dordrecht: Nijhoff, 1987.

MOSS, Ann. *Renaissance Truth and the Latin Language Turn*. Oxford: Oxford University Press, 2003.

NEWTON, Isaac. *Philosophical Writings* (Andrew Janiak ed.). Cambridge: Cambridge University Press, 2004.

PASCAL, Blaise. *Pensées* (H. F. Stewart trans.). New York: Pantheon, 1950.

PERROTTA, Annalisa. *I cristiani e gli altri: Guerre di religione, politica e propaganda nel poema cavalleresco di fine quattrocento*. Rome: Bagatto, 2017.

PULCI, Luigi. *Morgante: The Epic Adventures of Orlando and his Giant Friend Morgante* (Joseph Tusiani trans.). Bloomington: Indiana University Press, 1998.

RABELAIS, François. *Gargantua and Pantagruel* (M. A. Screech trans. and ed.). London: Penguin, 2006.

RODDA, Giordano. 'I maccheroni di Anton Francesco Doni'. *Giornale storico della letteratura italiana* 190(630): 185–211.

TAVONI, Mirko. *Il Quattrocento*. Bologna: Il Mulino, 1992.

ZOPPI, Federica. 'Zucche e antri infernali: considerazioni metaletterarie tra Folengo e Cervantes'. *Orillas: Rivista d'Ispanistica* 2: 1–29.